DOGS & PUPPIES

DOGS & PUPPIES

BARNES & NOBLE BOOKS

NEW YORK

This edition published by Barnes & Noble, Inc.,
by arrangement with Book Sales, Inc.

2004 Barnes & Noble Books

This edition produced for sales in the U.S.A., its
territories, and dependencies only.

M 10 9 8 7 6 5 4 3 2 1

ISBN 0-7607-6230-9

This book was designed and produced by
Quintet Publishing Limited
6 Blundell Street
London N7 9BH

Creative Director: Richard Dewing
Art Director: Lucy Parissi
Designer: James Lawrence
Project Editor: Clare Hubbard
Editor: Sylvia Goulding

Typeset in Great Britain by
Central Southern Typesetters, Eastbourne
Manufactured in Singapore by Eray Scan Pte Ltd.
Printed in Singapore by Star Standard Industries Pte Ltd.

CONTENTS

INTRODUCTION

Before buying a dog, it is essential to get as much information as possible about all the different breeds in order to help you select the right dog, not only in terms of looks and size, but also character and temperament.

Ownership of a dog is a serious undertaking. It requires a long-term commitment, bearing in mind that some breeds, the Miniature Poodle for instance, may live for 17 years or more. Twelve years is the average canine lifespan, during which time the dog must be fed, exercised, and groomed, receive veterinary attention for accidents and illnesses, and be taken into consideration whenever its owner is planning to be away from home for more than a matter of hours.

A long-term commitment

Many dog owners do not take such a responsible attitude. This does not mean that they are bad or uncaring. More likely, they made the decision to buy a dog in the belief that the requirements and temperament of one canine were much the same as another, and that the only consideration was whether the dog looked big and tough or small, cute, and cuddly. Yet some big, macho-looking dogs are great big softies, and some small breeds are famed for ill-humor. Only by

The relationship between human and dog is unique. If loved and well looked after, a dog will give its owner a lifetime of affection.

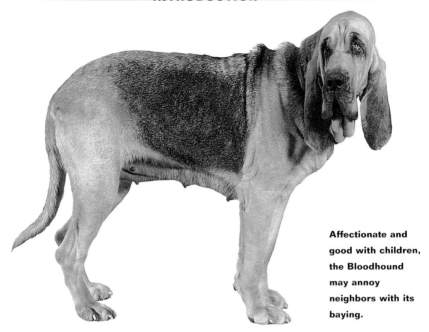

Affectionate and good with children, the Bloodhound may annoy neighbors with its baying.

studying the characteristics of different breeds can you find out which ones are really suitable for you.

In addition, before buying a dog you must make sure, unless you own your home, that the landlord does not object to its presence. Most standard leases preclude the keeping of pets without the written consent of the landlord.

The therapeutic value of dogs is being increasingly recognized—indeed there is an International Association of Human-Animal Interaction Organizations—with dogs playing their part in comforting residents in hospices and nursing homes, as hospital visitors (Pro-Active Therapy Dogs), and as Hearing Dogs for the Deaf. At the same time, however, the laws concerning dogs are becoming ever more stringent, with some breeds being outlawed in certain states and countries. Laws relating to dog ownership vary from state to state in the USA.

There is, for example, a very strict "poop and scoop" law in operation in New York State; elsewhere the number of dogs that any individual may keep is limited.

If you think much of this legislation is unnecessary, bear in mind that up to 10,000 cats and dogs are born every hour in the USA and that 200,000 animals pass through the hands of the American Society for the Prevention of Cruelty to Animals each year. For this reason alone it is vital to make the right initial choice, so that the partnership between dog and owner is a happy, long-lasting, and mutually beneficial one.

IDENTIFYING DOGS

People have known for more than 2,000 years that, by selective breeding, they could produce dogs that were not only a desired color and size, but which had inbred characteristics, for example strong guarding instincts or keen eyesight. Now you can learn to recognize the different physical and mental characteristics of over 100 dog breeds with this superb illustrated guide.

Parts of the dog

A special vocabulary has been developed to standardize the way in which the world's breeds are described.

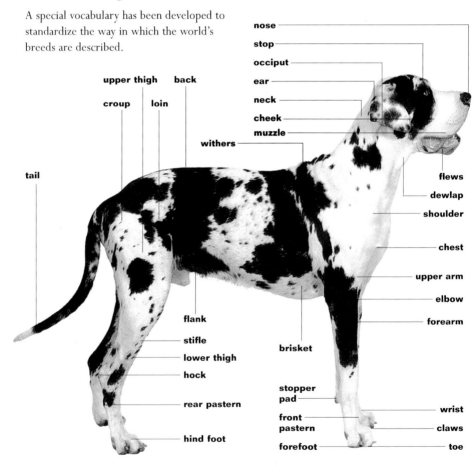

upper thigh

croup

back

loin

tail

withers

nose

stop

occiput

ear

neck

cheek

muzzle

flews

dewlap

shoulder

chest

upper arm

elbow

forearm

flank

stifle

lower thigh

hock

brisket

stopper pad

front pastern

forefoot

rear pastern

hind foot

wrist

claws

toe

GAIT

The term gait refers to the pattern of a dog's footsteps at various speeds; various types of gait are distinguishable by a particular rhythm and footfall.

Amble A relaxed, easy movement, often seen as a transition between the walk and the faster movements. The front and hind legs on either side move in unison.

Trot A slightly faster, rhythmic, two-beat, diagonal gait during which the feet at diagonally opposite corners of the body strike the ground together.

Canter A gait which has three beats to each stride. Two legs move separately and two as a diagonal pair. The movement is reminiscent of a rocking-horse, slower than a gallop, and not nearly so fatiguing.

Gallop The fastest gait, during which all four feet are off the ground at the same time.

Pace Movement or gait during which the left foreleg and left hind leg go forward in unison, followed by the right foreleg and right hind leg.

Hackney Almost identical to the action of the Hackney horse or pony, with the same high lifting of the front feet.

There are a number of faults in movement. Crabbing is where the dog moves with its body at an angle to the line of travel. Other names for this type of action are sidewinding, sidewheeling, and yawing. Cow-hocking is where the hocks turn inwards, facing one another. Dishing is similar to weaving in the horse, and is an unnatural movement of the forequarters.

BITE

A dog's bite is defined by the position of the lower jaw relative to the upper jaw.

 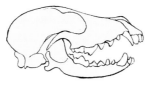 

NORMAL
Also called the scissor bite, where the upper and lower rows of teeth meet up.

OVERSHOT
A short lower jaw, and where the lower incisors (front teeth) protrude beyond the inner surface of the upper incisors.

UNDERSHOT
A long lower jaw, with the incisors projecting beyond those of the upper jaw.

EYES

The terminology for eyes is based on the shape of the eyes and how they are set in the skull. Because of the size of the muzzle, dogs have little overlapping sight, that is, they have only a small field of vision covered by both eyes. In breeds like the Bulldog, the eyes are positioned relatively far forward, limiting their total field of vision to 200 degrees.

Almond

Circular

Deep set

Globular

Goggly (round and protruding)

Haw (third membrane in the inside corner of the eye)

Oblique

Pig (very small and hard)

Triangular

HEADS

Within all dog breeds there are three basic skull types, which are further divided into subtypes. Eight typical subtypes, featured in the Dog Identifier section, are illustrated below. Heads lacking in refinement are termed "coarse."

Apple **Balanced** **Blocky** **Clean**

Egg-shaped **Otter** **Pear** **Rectangular**

COLORS

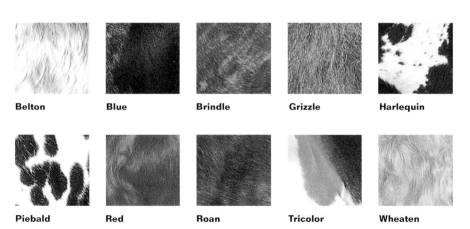

Belton **Blue** **Brindle** **Grizzle** **Harlequin**

Piebald **Red** **Roan** **Tricolor** **Wheaten**

EARS

A dog's ears are described in terms of their shape and how they hang from the head. The phrase "set on" refers to the position of the ears in relation to eye level and/or the width of the skull. Nine standard ear types are illustrated.

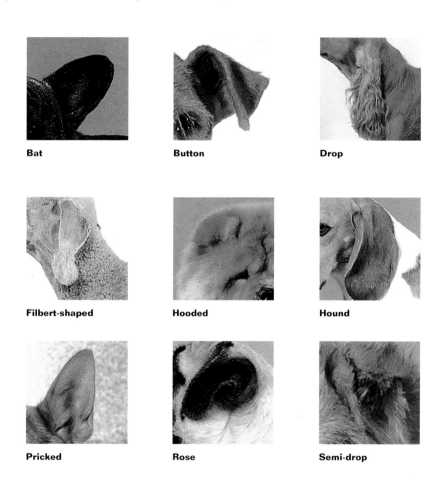

Bat

Button

Drop

Filbert-shaped

Hooded

Hound

Pricked

Rose

Semi-drop

TAILS

The names given to tails refer to their length, shape, position, and hair covering. The "tail set" refers to the way in which its base is set on the rump, whereas how the tail is "set on" refers to its placement—high, low, and so on. About 45 breeds have docked, or shortened, tails. The operation is usually performed by a veterinarian.

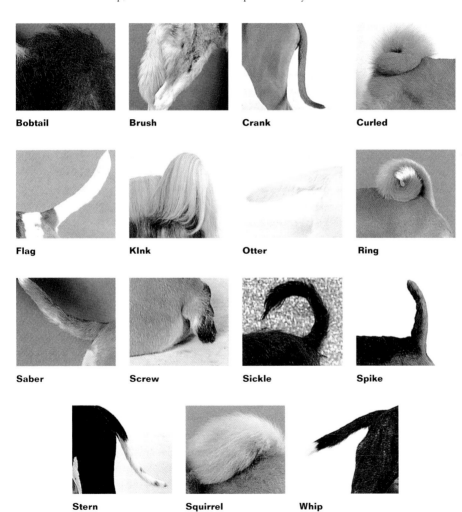

Bobtail

Brush

Crank

Curled

Flag

Klnk

Otter

Ring

Saber

Screw

Sickle

Spike

Stern

Squirrel

Whip

BREED GROUPS

Breeding for appearance was introduced in the 19th century. Up to that time, dog breeding concentrated on producing traits that were useful for work: vermin hunting (terriers), flushing and driving game (pointers, hounds), running down large and small quarry (mastiffs, greyhounds), and guarding (mastiffs).
Characteristics such as size, color, or set of tail can be introduced or altered by breeding from animals with those traits. It is also possible to introduce a feature from another breed—for example, Dingo blood added to the Smooth-coated Collie to produce the Australian Kelpie—and then to breed across enough generations for the trait to run "true."

NON-SPORTING DOGS

This is the category from which many pet dogs are selected. The breeds within this group are now the dogs whose sole purpose in life is to be a companion to their owners. Examples: Dalmatian, French Bulldog, Chow Chow (above)

WORKING DOGS

This group covers the traditional guards and workers, such as the Rottweiler (below). Bred to work, and in many cases fearsome, natural guards, most are happiest when they are doing the job for which they are bred.

HERDING DOGS

The breeds in this group were originally developed to herd and protect sheep and cattle. Many are still used by shepherds and farmers, but they are also extremely adaptable as pets. Examples: Collie, Corgi, German Shepherd Dog (below)

GUNDOGS

Gundogs are used variously to detect, flush out, and retrieve game. Usually gentle natured, many dogs in this category have the dual role of huntsman's dog and family pet. Examples: Pointer, Golden Retriever (above)

HOUNDS

Some hounds hunt by scent, some rely on their keen eyesight. Hounds are good natured but have a propensity to roam. Many hounds are kept in packs, in outside kennels, rather than living indoors. Examples: Greyhound, Basset, Bloodhound, Beagle (below)

TERRIERS

These dogs were bred to go to ground, to hunt vermin, and bolt the fox from its lair. Energetic, sporting, and sometimes noisy, most terriers are affectionate by nature, but they can nip. Example: Yorkshire Terrier (above)

TOY DOGS

Although traditionally regarded as lap dogs many toy breeds come within this category, and will walk their owners off their feet. Many are splendid guards, keenly intelligent, affectionate, if somewhat possessive, and courageous to the point of stupidity. Examples: Pomeranian (below), Chihuahua

CHOOSING A DOG

Dogs fulfill a wide range of working roles. The temperaments of certain breeds make them more or less suited to particular jobs, but good training will bring out the best in any dog.

First of all, it is important that the decision to buy a dog as well as the choice of breed has the approval of all those affected. It is important that, if you are closeted in an office every day, you do not rush out and buy a large hunting dog, which you expect someone else to look after when they had been secretly yearning for a Pekingese.

Secondly, never buy a dog on face value. Always check whether its abilities, temperament, and requirements are suitable for the role that you have in mind, and your

Army, police forces, and security guards around the world are using dogs to defend, search and, if necessary, attack.

circumstances. For instance, you may live in an apartment or a house, in the town or in the country, and your choice of breed should take this into account. In the case of a large, powerful breed or one that needs a great deal of exercise, you must be certain that you and your partner have the physical strength to control it.

By now you will have realized that study of the canine groups helps the dog buyer choose the best suited dog. In each case, you should find a number of varieties from which to make a choice. It should not be too difficult to find several breeds which, for

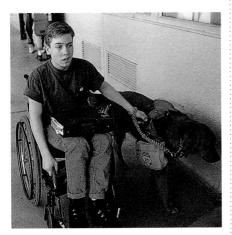

The right dog can become a loyal companion and provide invaluable assistance to disabled people.

example, combine the role of sporting dog and guard with that of a family pet, or which could, if you wish, be kenneled in the yard—while most pet dogs share their owners' home, many large, thick-coated dogs come to no harm outside. However, having kept your dog indoors for any time, it would be unkind to reverse that decision and subject it to the rigors of kennel life.

A wise decision

In talking to breeders, you are sure to be told that their type of dog is the right one for you. Similarly, one person will tell you, for example, that he would never keep a German Shepherd Dog in the same house as a child, while someone else will say that he would trust that dog with the child's life.

It is important to bear in mind that, in common with a number of other working dogs such as the Doberman and the Rottweiler, the German Shepherd is a natural

Herding dogs still work on many farms, protecting cattle and sheep. Many have also become family pets.

guard. Incidents reported in the media involving these breeds may well occur because these guarding breeds, which are naturally on the alert, misinterpreted a situation and sprang—as they saw it—to the defense of their charge. In other words, they did the job for which they were bred.

Don't force your dog to live in an unsuitable climate— some breeds are exceptionally sensitive to cold or heat.

UNDERSTANDING YOUR DOG

The surest way to develop a feel for your dog is by observing puppies in the nest.
The dog is a pack animal with a fundamental need for hierarchy.
Already at four to five weeks it is obvious which of the litter is most
dominant and how that dominance is asserted. This pup is the first to feed,
to initiate play, and to venture from the nest.
In leaving the litter, a puppy acquires a new pack, consisting of all the
members—human and animal—of its owner's household. It is at this time
that the handler establishes himself as the pack-leader.

Dog talk

As a dog matures, it develops a full repertoire of postures and signals to do with behavior. The confident dog conveys its non-aggressive dominance in its four-square posture, its ears erect, and tail held high. On meeting it, a dog which is less robust psychologically signals its submission by lowering its tail, flattening its ears, and perhaps turning its head to one side to avoid eye contact. In total submission, it may lie on its back.

Most canine signals—from the gaily wagging tail to the fearsome snarl—are easily read, but there are some which may be misinterpreted. Yawning, for instance: this is not a sign of tiredness but of confusion. The dog yawns because it is receiving conflicting signals. Staring is often a warning of impending attack and many people have provoked aggression by trying to master a dog with a stare.

Going on instinct

Whatever its nature or disposition, a dog's behavior is driven by instinct, not by intelligence as we understand it. The dog's intelligence is to do with instant perception, not with planning and foresight, and the differences in performance between breeds reflect inbred traits rather than intelligence.

The Border Collie, for instance, is unrivaled as a herding dog—a role for which it has been selectively bred over many generations. There is no reason why the collie cannot also be taught to retrieve to the gun but it will never do so with the same style and consistency as the retriever bred for this purpose.

The dog is a predator and its instincts are to hunt, guard, and reproduce. It is by channeling the first two of these drives (and controlling the third) that human beings have been able to forge such successful relationships with their dogs.

READING THE SIGNS

An aggressive stance

A sign of confusion

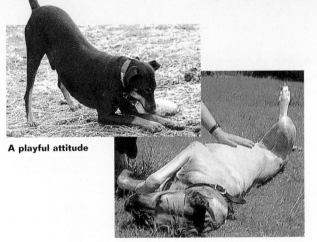

A playful attitude

Total submission

CARING FOR YOUR DOG

The cost element does come into dog-keeping, the larger breeds costing considerably more to maintain, in food terms, than the smaller—a toy breed will eat approximately 25 percent less than a Great Dane. The dog in regular work will also consume more food than its fellow that leads an indolent life, so this, too, must be taken into consideration. The breed standards laid down by national kennel clubs indicate, in many cases, the desired weight of the breed. If you are concerned that your dog falls below, or above, this ideal, you should consult your veterinarian, who may recommend a special diet.

Feeding

Caring for a new puppy

Young puppies, in particular, have voracious appetites. Their growth rate is at its peak during the first six months of life, so a sufficient intake of food is essential to produce the energy required for healthy development.

When you collect your pup from the breeder, they will normally hand you a diet sheet, which you should observe for the first months of the pup's life. You may not wish to continue feeding the recommended products, but it would be foolish to deviate from the breeder's recommendations until the pup is well grown. As the dogs grow, you can reduce the number of meals per day.

How much food?

The table right shows the quantity of food required by the different sizes of dog in the first twelve months of life.

Young puppies need several small meals per day.

Number of meals per day at age in months	Weaning 0-3	3-6	6-12
TOY (less than 10 lb)	3–5 oz	7 oz–1 lb 5 oz	11 oz–1$\frac{3}{4}$ lb
SMALL (10–20 lb)	7–12 oz	12 oz–1$\frac{3}{4}$ lb	1 lb 10 oz–2 lb
MEDIUM (20–50 lb)	12 oz–1 lb 5 oz	1 lb 9 oz–2 lb 3 oz	1 lb 14 oz–3$\frac{1}{2}$ lb
LARGE (50–75 lb)	1 lb 5 oz–1 lb 14 oz	1$\frac{3}{4}$ lb–3$\frac{1}{2}$ lb	3$\frac{1}{2}$ lb–4 lb 6 oz

These food and water bowls are perhaps a little large for this poodle pup.

Grooming

Most people have a preference for a long- or a short-coated animal, and even sometimes for a particular color. Remember, however, that the long-coated animal is likely to need far more time spent on grooming than the short-coated one, and that the light-colored dog, for instance the Dalmatian, is going to shed hairs that will be apparent on the living-room carpet.

What are the requirements of each breed of dog? The majority of fanciers are only expert in preparing their own chosen breed, and perhaps one or two others. Only professional dog groomers could, for example, advise on the bathing, trimming, scissoring, and grooming of all the breeds recognized by the American Kennel Club.

Special effects

While quite a number of breeds have to be hand-stripped, using fingers and/or a stripping knife, to give the coat the desired effect for the show ring, these same breeds are often clipped instead when they are kept solely as domestic pets.

The Bouvier des Flandres requires only little grooming.

This "before and after" picture shows how much work is required even on a small dog like the Bichon Frise.

Smooth-coated breeds such as the American Staffordshire Terrier, Boston Terrier, and French Bulldog need only be groomed every day or two using a short, bristle brush; the German Shepherd Dog, and many of the spaniels and retrievers, need daily grooming using a bristle brush and a comb; those breeds that need particular coat care and regular visits to the grooming parlor for clipping, stripping, and perhaps, scissoring, include the Airedale Terrier, the Schnauzers, and the Poodles.

It must be emphasized, therefore, that, if time and expense are a consideration, you would be well advised to think in terms of a smooth, short-coated breed.

The Yorkshire Terrier is a first-class show dog for those with the time to spare for intricate grooming.

Space

You will need to be aware of the space requirements of the dog you choose. Obviously, the Dachshund is a good choice for a small house or apartment as it requires only limited living space, while the Otterhound needs a lot of room. Perhaps surprisingly, however, space requirements are not entirely dependent on the dog's size—the tiny Pekingese needs to have a good amount of space to move about in, while the large Greyhound, for example, is accustomed during its racing life to occupying a confined area away from the track, and will happily relax in its own corner when in a domestic situation.

Exercise

The amount of exercise required by each breed again varies enormously. It is vital that you check in advance whether you can give the dog sufficient freedom to roam and run. Leaving a lively dog like the Siberian Husky cooped up is cruel, while the fierce-looking Bulldog is quite happy with only short walks.

Keeping your Dog Healthy

Ask the breeder about the pup's worming program and check whether it has had any inoculations against killer diseases such as canine distemper and parvo virus. If not, you will need to arrange for the necessary shots with your veterinarian and to establish the routine for annual booster shots thereafter.

Finally, if the pup that you have chosen is registered with its national kennel club, the breeder should give you its Certificate of Pedigree. Make sure that this has been duly signed and completed, so that you can arrange official transfer of ownership into your name.

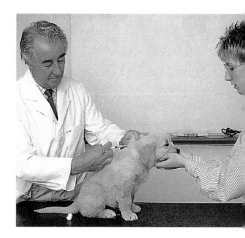

Inoculation against the common canine diseases is vital to keep your dog in good health.

DOG IDENTIFIER

This book is user-friendly. The breeds are arranged in groups—non-sporting dogs, working dogs, herding dogs, gundogs, hounds, terriers, and toy dogs.

Key to Symbols

| Food | Grooming | Space | Exercise |

Each breed is accompanied by symbols which provide you with at-a-glance information on this dog's specific needs and requirements. The four categories—food, grooming, space, and exercise—are each divided into four grades. Within the exercise category, for example, one quarter shaded indicates that little exercise is required, while total shading indicates the need for a great deal of exercise.

NON-SPORTING DOGS

Boston Terrier

The Boston Terrier, formerly the **American Bull Terrier, derives from a crossbred Bulldog/Terrier that was imported into the United States from Britain in 1865. Barnard's Tom, the first example of the breed with the desired screw tail, was bred in Boston, Massachusetts, and registered with the American Kennel Club in 1893. The breed takes its name from the city where it was developed.**

Coat Short and smooth.
Color Brindle with white markings: brindle must show distinctly throughout body; black with white markings, but brindle with white markings preferred.
Features Square head, flat on top; round eyes set wide apart; broad, square jaw; ears erect at corners of head; broad chest; fine, low-set tail.
Size Weight not exceeding 25 lb divided by classes:
    Lightweight under 15 lb;
    Middleweight under 20 lb;
    Heavyweight under 25 lb.
Care It is easy to look after and requires little grooming. However, it is difficult to obtain a show specimen with the right markings—ideally, a white muzzle, even a white blaze over the head and down the collar, breast, and forelegs, below elbows.

Character It is a lively, intelligent dog, and a loving family pet. A joy to have around the house, it is nevertheless determined and self willed.

The lively and intelligent Boston Terrier is a compactly built, well-balanced dog with a rather short body.

The Boston Terrier's head should be in proportion to its size; its teeth should be short and regular, with an even bite, and its neck of fair length, slightly arched, carrying the dog's head gracefully.

Bulldog

The Bulldog's proud ancestry can be traced back to the Molussus, the fighting dog named from an ancient Greek tribe, the Molossi. As its name suggests, it was bred to bait bulls.

Coat Short, smooth, and close, and finely textured.
Color Uniform color or with black mask or muzzle; reds, red brindle, piebald; black undesirable.
Features Large skull; eyes set low; ears small and set high on head; broad, sloping shoulders; tail set low and can be either straight or screwed.
Size Weight: dogs 50–55 lb, bitches 40–50 lb.
Care The only grooming it requires is a daily run through with a stiff brush, and a rub-down. Care must be taken that it is not over-exerted in hot weather.

The Bulldog's shoulders are broad, sloping, and deep. They are also very powerful and muscular, giving the appearance of having been tacked on to its body.

Character Despite its fearsome appearance, the Bulldog is a gentle, good-natured dog. It adores children and makes a delightful pet.

French Bulldog

The French Bulldog is a descendant of small bulldogs, but it is not known whether these were of English or Spanish stock. It became a popular breed in the early 1900s.

Coat Short, smooth, close, and finely textured.

Color Brindle, pied, or fawn.

Features Head square, large, and broad; eyes dark and set wide apart; "bat ears," broad at base and rounded at tip, set high and carried upright; body short, muscular, and cobby; tail very short.

Size Average height: 12 in. Weight:dogs about 28 lb, bitches 24 lb.

Care The "Frenchie" is easy to groom, requiring just a daily brush and a rub-down with a piece of toweling to make its coat shine. The facial creases should be lubricated to prevent soreness. This breed should not be exercised in hot weather.

Character Makes a delightful companion. It is good-natured, affectionate, and courageous, and usually gets on well with children and with other pets. Owners must become accustomed to its gentle snuffling, and be aware that it will invariably wander off and sulk on the rare occasions when it is in disgrace.

The French Bulldog is gentle and peace-loving. It has distinctive "bat" ears and a natural screw tail.

Dalmatian

Named after Dalmatia on the Adriatic coast, the Dalmatian was established in Britain, where it was popular as a carriage dog.

Coat Short, fine, dense, and close; sleek and glossy in appearance.
Color Pure white ground color with black or liver brown spots, round and well-defined, and as evenly distributed as possible; spots on extremities smaller than those on body.
Features Long head and flat skull; eyes set moderately far apart; medium-size ears set high; deep chest; long tail that is carried with a slight upward curve.

Size Height at withers: 19–23 in. Weight: 50–55 lb.
Care Requires plenty of exercise and a daily brushing but does tend to shed white hairs, which does not endear the breed to the houseproud.
Character This affectionate and energetic dog quickly becomes a family favorite. Intelligent and equable temperament.

A friendly, outgoing dog capable of great speed. The Dalmatian should be free of any aggression or nervousness.

The nose of the black-spotted Dalmatian is always black, but in the liver-spotted variety it is brown.

German Spitz

There are many varieties of spitz and, although it is difficult to pinpoint their origin, they were probably brought from Scandinavia by the Vikings. Spitz dogs were known as early as 1700 when white specimens were said to be kept in Pomerania and black ones in Württemberg.

Coat Soft, woolly undercoat and long, dense, straight outer coat.
Color All solid color varieties.
Features A broad head; oval-shape eyes; small, triangular ears; compact body; tail set on high and carried curled over the body.

Size *Small* Height: 9–11 in.
Standard Height: 11½–13 in.
Care Can adapt to life in the town or country, and needs vigorous daily brushing and an average amount of exercise.
Character This active, intelligent, and alert dog is independent, yet devotion to its human family is a breed characteristic. If unchecked, it does have a tendency to yap.

The confident German Spitz should never show any sign of nervousness or aggression. Indeed, its buoyancy, independence, and devotion to its human family are the breed characteristics.

Japanese Spitz

The Japanese Spitz shares ancestry with the Nordic Spitz and is also closely related to the German Spitz. It is a family favorite in Japan.

Coat Straight, dense, stand-off outer coat; thick, short, dense undercoat.
Color Pure white.
Features Medium-size head; dark eyes; small triangular ears standing erect; broad, deep chest; tail set on high and carried curled over back.

Size Height at shoulders: dogs 12–14 in; bitches slightly smaller. Average weight: 13 lb.
Care Requires daily brushing and enjoys a fair amount of exercise.
Character Loyal to its owners but distrustful of strangers, this beautiful Spitz is alert, intelligent, lively, and bold. It makes a fine small guard.

Finnish Spitz

The Finnish Spitz was once used by Lapp hunters to track elk and polar bears, but is now popular throughout Scandinavia for hunting grouse and other game birds.

Coat Short and close on head and front of legs, longer on body and back of legs; semi-erect and stiff on neck and back.

Color Reddish-brown or red-gold on back, preferably bright.

Features Medium-size head and eyes; ears small and cocked, and sharply pointed; body almost square in outline; tail plumed, and curves vigorously from the root.

Size Height at withers: dogs 17–20 in, bitches 15–18 in. Weight: 25–35 lb.

Care Requires plenty of exercise and daily brushing.

Character The Finnish Spitz is appreciated as a faithful companion and home-loving pet, which is good with children.

Keeshond

Like other spitz breeds, the Keeshond (pronounced "kayshond") is believed to derive from an Arctic breed. It became popular in Holland as the companion of barge-dwellers and as a watchdog.

Coat Long and straight with the hairs standing out; a dense ruff over the neck.
Color A mixture of gray, black, and cream; undercoat pale.

Features Well-proportioned head that is wedge-shaped when seen from above; dark, medium-size eyes; small, triangular ears; compact body; well-feathered, high-set tail that curls tightly over the back.
Size Height at shoulders: dogs, about 18 in, bitches 17 in. Weight: 55–66 lb.
Care Requires daily grooming using a stiff brush, and a fair amount of exercise. A choke chain will spoil the ruff.
Character Good natured and long-lived, the Keeshond tends to be a devoted, one-person dog.

Chow Chow

A member of the spitz family, the Chow Chow has been known in its native China for more than 2000 years. It is the only dog with a black tongue.

Coat Can be rough—abundant, dense, and coarse, with pronounced ruff around head and neck, and feathering on tail; or smooth—dense and hard.

Color Black, red, blue, fawn, and cream.

Features Broad, flat head; dark, almond-shape eyes; small ears slightly rounded at tips; long, nicely arched neck; broad, deep chest and compact body; tail set on high and carried curled over the back.

Size Height at shoulders: dogs 19–22 in, bitches 18–20 in. Weight: 45–70 lb.

Care A daily walk; the full coat requires considerable attention with a wire brush.

Character The Chow Chow has always had a reputation for ferocity but it is unlikely to attack unless provoked. It is a faithful, odor-free dog, which makes a good pet; it needs firm but gentle handling.

A former hunter of wolves, the Chow Chow is a good guard.

Shiba Inu

The Shiba Inu is an ancient Japanese breed—remains of a dog of this type were found in ruins dating back to 500 BC. It is the smallest of the spitz dogs, and its name means "little dog" in the Nagano dialect.

Coat Harsh, straight.
Color Red, salt and pepper, black, black and tan, or white.

Features Agile, sturdily built, and well muscled; deep chest; long back; almond-shape eyes; long sickle tail.
Size Height at shoulders: dogs 15–16 in, bitches 14–15 in. Weight: 20–30 lb.
Care Needs a fair amount of exercise and a good daily brushing to keep it looking trim.
Character The Shiba is an affectionate, friendly, and sensitive dog that makes a fine pet as well as a show dog and/or hunter.

Schnauzer

The Schnauzer or Standard Schnauzer is the oldest of the three varieties of Schnauzer. It was originally used as an all-purpose farm dog, and was a good ratter. It is also an excellent companion.

Coat Harsh and wiry, with a soft undercoat.
Color Pure black (white markings on head, chest, and legs undesirable), or pepper and salt.
Features Strong head of a good length; dark, oval-shape eyes; neat, pointed ears; chest moderately broad; tail set on and carried high, and is characteristically docked to three joints.

Size Standard height at shoulders: dogs 18½–19½ in, bitches 17½–18½ in. Weight: around 33 lb.
Care Enjoys plenty of exercise, and its hardy, harsh, wiry coat needs a certain amount of stripping and plucking. Pet dogs can be clipped but this will spoil the coat for showing.
Character The Schnauzer is an attractive, robust, intelligent, and playful dog, which makes a good companion, and is generally good with children.

The Schnauzer's movement should be free, balanced, and vigorous.

Miniature Schnauzer

The Miniature Schnauzer, known in its native Germany as the Zwerg-schnauzer, was derived from crossing the Standard Schnauzer with smaller dogs. In the United States and Canada, the Miniature Schnauzer is classed as a terrier, and it was at one time the most popular terrier there.

Coat Harsh, hard, and wiry.
Color Pure black, or pepper and salt.
Features Strong head of a good length; dark, oval-shape eyes; neat, pointed ears; tail is set on and carried high, and is normally docked to three joints.
Size Height: 12–14 in. Weight: 13–15 lb.
Care Like its larger contemporaries, it needs a fair amount of exercise and its coat should be periodically stripped and plucked. The coat may also be clipped.
Character The Miniature Schnauzer is a delightful small dog, an excellent family pet and children's companion.

Giant Schnauzer

The Giant Schnauzer, or Riesenschnauzer, worked as a cattle dog until the need for such an animal declined. Not as popular as the Standard and Miniature varieties, the Giant Schnauzer might have become extinct had it not proved itself an excellent guard dog in the First World War. However, it was not until after the Second World War that the deserved popularity was secured for this fine dog.

Coat Harsh, hard, and wiry.

Color Pure black, or pepper and salt.

Features Strong head of a good length; dark, oval-shape eyes; neat, pointed ears; chest moderately broad; tail is set on and carried high, and is characteristically docked to three joints.

Size Shoulder height: dogs 25½–27¼ in, bitches 23½–25½ in.

Weight: 73–77 lb.

Care Regular stripping prevents the prized "hard coat" of the Giant Schnauzer from becoming soft and woolly.

Character This intelligent dog makes a reliable, good-natured companion, which requires a fair amount of exercise.

Miniature Poodle

The Miniature Poodle, bred down from the Standard by using smaller specimens, became the most popular breed during the 1950s.

Coat Very profuse and dense.
Color All solid colors; clear colors preferred in show dogs.
Features Long, fine head; almond-shape eyes; ears set on high and hanging close to head; chest deep and broad; tail set on high and carried up.
Size Height at shoulders: 10–15 in. Weight: 26–31 lb.
Care Requires frequent regular visits to the canine beauty parlor. Use a wire-pin pneumatic brush and a wire-toothed metal comb for daily grooming.
Character Intelligent and fun-loving.

Standard Poodle

Known in France as the *Caniche*, the Poodle was favored by the French Queen Marie Antoinette (1755–93). However, it originated in Germany as a water retriever, or *Pudel*. It resembles the Irish Water Spaniel, and both share common ancestors.

Coat Very profuse and dense: a good, harsh texture.
Color Solid colors; clear preferred.
Features Long, fine head; almond-shape eyes; ears set on high and hanging close to head: chest deep and broad; tail set on high and carried up.
Size Height at shoulders: over 15 in. Weight: 45–70 lb.
Care Whatever style of clipping you choose, you will need to use a wire-pin pneumatic brush and a wire-toothed metal comb for daily grooming. Even the pet Poodle must attend the canine beauty parlor every six weeks or so.
Character The Standard Poodle still retains its ability as a gundog and swims well. Its intelligence and eagerness to learn mean that it is popular in obedience trials and as a circus dog.

This happy, good-tempered, lively dog makes a good family pet, enjoying a fair amount of exercise. It is also a fine show dog, provided you have the time for intricate preparation. While it is shown in the lion clip, many pet owners prefer the lamb clip (with hair uniform length).

The Poodle does not
molt. Its woolly coat
does not usually affect
asthma sufferers.

Toy Poodle

A descendent of the Miniature Poodle, the Toy Poodle is the least robust of the three varieties, so it is essential to select from sound stock.

Coat Profuse and dense; harsh texture.
Color All solid colors; clear colors are generally preferred.
Features Long, fine head; almond-shape eyes; ears set on high; chest deep and broad; tail set on high and carried up.

Size Height at shoulders: under 10 in. Weight: 15 lb.
Care Requires regular visits to the canine beauty parlor. Use a wire-pin pneumatic brush and a wire-toothed metal comb for daily grooming.
Character The Toy Poodle is happy and good tempered, and makes a delightful pet that is ideal for the apartment dweller who nonetheless enjoys a canine companion.

Bichon Frise

Like the Poodle, the Bichon Frise is thought to be a descendant of the French water dog, the Barbet, and its name comes from the dimunitive, *barbichon*. Friendly and outgoing, this little dog has grown steadily in popularity since the late 1970s.

Coat Long and loosely curling.

Color White, cream, or apricot markings permissible up to 18 months. Dark skin considered desirable.

Features Long ears hanging close to head; dark, round eyes with black rims; relatively long, arched neck; tail carried gracefully curved over the body.

Size Height at withers: 9–11 in.

Care The Bichon Frise has to have its coat regularly scissored. It is often to be seen in a canine beauty parlor.

Character Happy, friendly, and lively, this breed makes an attractive and cuddly small pet, which will enjoy as much exercise as most owners can provide.

Shar-Pei

At one time the rarest dog in the
world, the Shar-Pei or Chinese
Fighting Dog dates back to the Han
Dynasty (206 BC to AD 220).

Coat Short, straight, and bristly; no
undercoat on loose skin.
Color Solid colors only—black, red, light
or dark fawn, or cream.

Features Head rather large in proportion
to body; dark, almond-shape eyes; very
small, triangular ears; broad, deep chest;
rounded tail narrowing to a fine point, set on
high and curling over to either side.
Size Height at withers: 18–20 in.
Weight: 40–55 lb.
Care Coat is never trimmed; needs a
reasonable amount of exercise.
Character A very affectionate dog with a
frowning expression, the Shar-Pei is calm,
independent and devoted.

Tibetan Terrier

The Tibetan Terrier is not really a terrier at all, having no history of going to earth. It resembles a small Old English Sheepdog and is said to have been bred in Tibetan monasteries for farmwork and as a companion.

Coat Soft, woolly undercoat; long, fine outer coat that can be straight or wavy.
Color Any color or combination of colors.
Features Large, round, dark eyes; pendant, feathered ears; compact and powerful body; medium-length tail set quite high and carried curled over the back.
Size Height at shoulders: dogs 14–16 in, bitches slightly smaller.
Average weight: 20–24 lb.
Care Long coat needs regular attention.
Character Loyal, sturdy, a good walker, and devoted to its owners and to children, but a little apprehensive of strangers.

Tibetan Spaniel

Unrelated to the spaniels, the Tibetan Spaniel is thought to have been in existence since the 7th century. Its origins are obscure.

Coat Moderately long and silky in texture; shorter on face and fronts of legs; feathering on ears, backs of legs and tail.
Color All solid colors and mixtures.

Features Head small in proportion to body; dark brown, expressive eyes; medium-size pendant ears; tail set on high, richly plumed, and carried curled over the back.
Size Height: 10 in. Weight: 9–15 lb.
Care Energetic; enjoys a good romp; coat needs regular grooming.
Character Intelligent, good with children; makes a splendid housepet.

Lhasa Apso

The Lhasa Apso, a small, indoor watchdog, originated in Tibet. The word *apso* means goat-like—its coat resembled that of the goats kept by Tibetan herders.

Coat Top coat long, heavy, straight, and hard. Moderate undercoat.

Color Solid golden, sandy, honey, dark grizzle, slate, or smoke; black parti-color, white, or brown; all equally acceptable.

Features Long hair on head covering eyes and reaching toward floor; heavily feathered ears; dark eyes; compact, well-balanced body; tail set on high, carried over back.

Size Height at shoulders: dogs about 10 in, bitches slightly smaller.

Care Enjoys a good romp outside; careful daily grooming of long coat needed.

Character The Lhasa Apso is happy, usually long-lived, adaptable, and good in families with children.

Shih Tzu

The Shih Tzu, whose Chinese name means "lion dog," is generally thought to have originated in western China. It resembles a Lhasa Apso except for its shortened face, and could be the result of crossing the Lhasa Apso and the Pekingese.

Coat Long, dense, with a good undercoat.
Color All colors permissible; white blaze on forehead, and white tip on tail highly desirable in parti-colors.

Features Broad, round head, wide between the eyes; large, dark, round eyes; large ears with long feathers, carried drooping; body longer between withers and root of tail than height at withers; tail heavily plumed and carried curved well over back.
Size Height at withers: 9–10½ in. Weight: 9–18 lb.
Care Requires a good daily grooming using a bristle brush, and the topknot is usually tied with a bow.
Character This happy, hardy little dog loves children and other animals, and makes a good housepet suited to town or country.

Schipperke

The Schipperke originated in Belgium, where it was once the most popular housepet and watchdog. Traditionally its job there was to guard canal barges when they were tied up for the night, and it was this task that earned the breed its name—*Schipperke* is Flemish for "little captain."

Coat Abundant and dense, with longer hair on the neck, shoulders, chest, and backs of rear legs.

Color Black, but the undercoat can be slightly lighter. Outside the USA other solid colors are permissible.

Features Broad head with flat skull; eyes oval, dark brown; ears moderately long: chest broad and deep; the tail is docked.

Size Height at withers: dogs 11–13 in, bitches 10–12 in. Weight: 12–18 lb.

Care Said to be able to walk up to 6 miles a day, but will make do with considerably less exercise; should be housed indoors rather than in a kennel.

Character The Schipperke is an affectionate dog which is good with children, usually very long lived, and an excellent watchdog.

WORKING DOGS

Mastiff

The Mastiff is among the most ancient breeds of dog, treasured by the Babylonians over 4000 years ago, and resident in Britain since the time of Julius Caesar. The breed has proved its worth as a formidable guard and as a hunter. After the Second World War numbers declined in America, but the situation is gradually improving.

Coat Outer coat short and straight; undercoat dense and close-lying.

Color Apricot, fawn, or brindle; in all, the muzzle, ears, and nose should be black, with black around the eyes and extending up between them.

Features Broad skull; small eyes set wide apart; small ears; long, broad body; legs squarely set; tail set on high.

Size Minimum height: dogs 30 in, bitches 27½ in. Weight: 175–190 lb.

Care Needs regular walking to build up its muscles. Many do not complete growth until their second year.

Character Of great strength and dignity, the Mastiff is normally gentle, but can be a formidable guard.

Large and dignified, the Mastiff is devoted to its owner.

Tibetan Mastiff

The Tibetan Mastiff is descended from a fighting dog of ancient Rome. It originated in central Asia, where it guarded flocks.

Coat Medium length, thicker on males than females, with a heavy undercoat.
Color Rich black, black and tan, brown, various shades of gold, various shades of gray, gray with gold markings.

Features Broad, heavy head; medium-size, very expressive eyes; medium-size ears; strong body with a straight back; tail medium length to long.
Size Minimum height: dogs 26 in, bitches 24 in. Minimum weight: 180 lb.
Care Needs regular vigorous exercise on hard ground, and daily brushing.
Character This breed makes a fine companion, watchdog, and guard. It is aloof, protective, and slow to mature. Reliable temperament unless provoked.

The tail of the Tibetan Mastiff curls over its back.

Bullmastiff

Developed some 200–300 years ago, the Bullmastiff is the result of a cross between the Mastiff and the British Bulldog. It was a brave fighting dog, which could bear pain without flinching, and had a considerable reputation for ferocity.

Coat Short, smooth, and dense.
Color Any shade of brindle, fawn, or red; a slight white marking on the chest is permissible, other white markings are undesirable; black muzzle.
Features Broad skull; small eyes set wide apart; small ears; long, broad body; legs squarely set; tail set on high.

Size Height at shoulders: dogs 25–27 in, bitches 24–26 in. Weight: dogs 110–130 lb, bitches 90–110 lb.
Care Needs grooming every few days.
Character Despite its ferocious past, the Bullmastiff of today is a playful, loyal, and gentle animal, an excellent guard, and usually very dependable with children. However, it is too powerful for a child or slight adult to control, and should only be kept by experienced dog owners.

The Bullmastiff is a handsome, but ferocious dog—not suitable as a children's companion.

Rottweiler

An ancient breed, which in the past worked as a draught dog delivering meat, a hunter of wild boar, and a trusted cattle dog. The Rottweiler is believed by some to be a descendant of the early German Shepherd Dog, while others consider that its ancestor was similar to the Tibetan Mastiff. More recently, the Rottweiler has proved itself to be an intelligent police dog and guard.

Coat Medium length, coarse, and lying flat, with undercoat on neck and thighs.
Color Black with clearly defined tan or deep brown markings.

Features Head broad between the ears; medium-size, almond-shape eyes, ears small in proportion to head; powerful, arched neck; broad, deep chest; tail docked at first joint and usually carried horizontally.
Size Height at shoulders: dogs 24–27 in, bitches 22–25 in. Weight: 90–110 lb.
Care Needs space and plenty of exercise; needs daily grooming with a bristle brush or hound glove and comb.
Character The Rottweiler is a large, courageous dog that makes an excellent companion-guard and responds to kindly but firm handling, but it should only be handled by experienced owners.

Courageous and loyal, the Rottweiler can be a fearsome guard which will attack without warning, but many are gentle pets.

Boxer

The Boxer traces back to the mastiff-type dogs taken into battle against the Romans by the Cimbrians, a Germanic tribe. Since the early 1900s, the breed has attained immense popularity worldwide.

Coat Short, glossy, and smooth.
Color Fawn or brindle with any white markings, not exceeding one-third of ground color.

Features Dark brown, forward-looking eyes; moderate-size ears set wide apart; body square in profile; tail set on high and characteristically docked.
Size Height: dogs 22½–25 in, bitches 21–23 in. Weight: 53–71 lb.
Care Needs a reasonable amount of exercise; short coat is easy to care for.
Character The Boxer is an affectionate, playful breed which retains puppyish ways well into maturity. It is kind with children, but not averse to a fight with its fellows. This obedient and loyal dog also makes a good guard.

A strong dog, the Boxer needs a considerable amount of exercise.

Canaan Dog

An indigenous breed of Israel, the Canaan has also proved its worth as a protector of livestock, guard dog, in the army, as a guide dog for the blind, and as a search and rescue dog.

Coat Medium to long, straight and harsh; undercoat visible in winter.

Color Sandy to reddish brown, white or black; harlequin also permissible.

Features Well-proportioned head; eyes slightly slanting; pricked ears; body generally strong; bushy tail set on high, carried curled over back when alert.

Size Height at withers: 19½–23½ in. Weight: 40–55 lb.

Care Needs regular grooming with a brush and comb.

Character The Canaan is alert, home loving, and loyal to its family, faithfully guarding those entrusted to its care.

Great Dane

The Great Dane, known in its native Germany as the Deutsche Dogge (German Mastiff), is a statuesque dog, often referred to as the Apollo of the dog world. It is said to be descended from the Molussus hounds of ancient Rome, and, in the Middle Ages, was used as a wild boar hunter, companion, and bodyguard.

Coat Short, dense, and sleek.
Color Brindle, fawn, blue, black, or harlequin (white, preferably with all black or all blue patches that have the appearance of being torn).
Features Large, wide, and open nostrils; fairly deep-set eyes; triangular ears; very deep body; long tail, thick at the root and tapering toward the tip.

Size Minimum height over 18 months: dogs 30 in, bitches 28 in. Minimum weight over 18 months: dogs 120 lb, bitches 100 lb.
Care Needs regular exercise on hard ground and daily grooming with a body brush. A sad fact for owners of this majestic breed is that it lives for only 8–9 years.
Character Despite its size, this breed should not be kenneled outside, but kept in the house as a member of the family. The Great Dane is good natured, playful, and easy to train. However, it should not be teased lest an action be misinterpreted.

One of the tallest dogs in the world, the Great Dane was a favorite of the German Chancellor Bismarck.

Komondor

Used for centuries to guard flocks and property on the Hungarian plains, the Komondor is hardy, healthy, and tolerant of changing temperatures. It can never be mistaken for any other dog because of its full white coat falling in tassels, or cords, which resembles an old-fashioned string mop.

Coat Long, coarse outer coat; curly or wavy; softer undercoat.
Color White.

Features Head is short; medium-size eyes and ears; muscular, slightly arched neck; broad, deep body with a muscular chest; level back; the tail is long and slightly curved at the tip.
Size Minimum height at withers: dogs 25 in, bitches 23½ in. Weight: 80–150 lb.
Care Needs plenty of exercise and meticulous grooming.
Character The Komondor will guard with its life sheep, cattle, or children. While utterly devoted to its human family, it is wary of strangers, does not take kindly to teasing, and may attack without warning.

Leonberger

A German breed, the Leonberger is generally thought to be a cross of a Landseer and a Pyrenean Mountain Dog. It has worked as a watchdog, a protector of livestock, and as a draught dog, and is today considered a rare breed.

Coat Medium soft, fairly long, and close to body.

Color Light yellow, golden to red-brown; preferably with black mask.

Features Top of head domed; eyes vary from light brown to brown; ears set high: long body; bushy tail carried at half-mast.

Size Height at withers: dogs 28–32 in, bitches 26–30 in. Weight: 80–150 lb.

Care Essentially a country dog, it needs daily brushing, regular exercise, and plenty of space.

Character Good natured, intelligent, and lively, the Leonberger is a fine-looking watchdog. It is very good with children, and has a great love of water.

Pyrenean Mountain Dog

The Pyrenean Mountain Dog has been used for centuries to guard flocks in the Pyrenean mountains bordering France and Spain, and throughout France.

Coat Long and coarse-textured, with a profuse undercoat of very fine hair.
Color White, with or without patches of badger, and wolf-gray or pale yellow.

Features Rounded crown; dark brown, almond-shape eyes; small, triangular ears; broad chest; level back; tail thick at root and tapering towards tip.
Size Height at withers: dogs 28–32 in, bitches 26–29 in. Minimum weight: dogs 110 lb, bitches 90 lb.
Care Can be kept in or out of doors, but must be well trained. Needs sufficient space, food, and regular exercise and brushing.
Character Generally good natured, gets on with other pets, and a faithful protector.

Saint Bernard

A gentle giant, the Saint Bernard is named after the Medieval Hospice of St Bernard, to which it was introduced in the 17th century. It is famous for rescuing travelers and climbers on the Swiss Alps.

Coat Dense, short, smooth, and lying close to body.

Color Orange, mahogany-brindle, red-brindle, or white, with patches on body in any of these colors; white on face, muzzle, collar, chest, forelegs, feet, and end of tail; black shadings on face and ears.

Features Massive, wide head with heavy dewlaps; medium-size eyes and ears; broad, muscular shoulders; broad, straight back; tail set on high.

Size Minimum height at shoulder: dogs 27½ in, bitches 23½ in. Weight: 110–200 lb.

Care Don't give too much exercise in the first year of life, short regular walks being better than long ones. Needs daily brushing and requires generous quantities of food. The Saint Bernard requires plenty of space. It also slobbers.

Character True to its past, the Saint Bernard is intelligent, eminently trainable, loves children, and is a kindly dog.

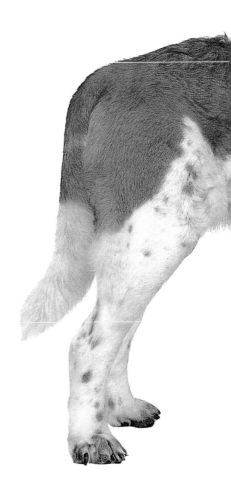

The Saint Bernard is intelligent, faithful, and extremely gentle. It loves children, too, but does require plenty of space and large food rations.

The white blaze that runs up the face of the Saint Bernard emphasizes its benevolent expression.

Bernese Mountain Dog

The Bernese Mountain Dog, named after the canton of Berne in Switzerland, has worked as herder and flock guardian, and is still used to pull milk carts up Swiss mountains.

Coat Thick, moderately long, and straight or slightly wavy, with a bright sheen.
Color Jet black, with rich, reddish brown markings on cheeks, over eyes, on legs and chest; some white markings.

Features Strong head with a flat skull; dark brown, almond-shape eyes; medium-size ears; compact body; bushy tail.
Size Height at withers: dogs 25–27½ in, bitches 23–26 in. Weight: about 88 lb.
Care Needs regular brushing, plenty of space and exercise.
Character The Bernese Mountain Dog makes a good pet, being amiable toward children and other pets.

Doberman

The Doberman was developed in Germany as a ferocious, short-coated dog with courage and stamina. It was developed from the German Pinscher, the Rottweiler, the Manchester Terrier, and possibly also the Pointer.

Coat Smooth, short, thick, and close.
Color Solid black, brown, blue, or fawn, with rust markings on head, body, and legs.

Features Almond-shape eyes; small neat ears set high on head; well-arched neck; square body; tail characteristically docked at second joint.
Size Height at withers: dogs 26–28 in, bitches 24–26 in. Weight: 66–88 lb.
Care Needs a lot of exercise, and should be groomed every couple of days.
Character The Doberman is obedient and can make a good family pet, but it needs knowledgeable handling and training, being constantly "on guard."

Constantly on the alert, the Doberman makes a first-class companion and guard.

Pinscher

The Pinscher ("biter," in German) has existed in Germany for several hundred years. The old Black and Tan Terrier may have contributed to its development. It resembles the larger Doberman, to which it contributed.

Coat Short and dense.
Color All colors, ranging from solid fawn to stag red; black or blue with reddish/tan markings.

Features Dark, medium-size eyes; V-shape ears set on high; wide chest; tail set on and carried high, and usually docked to three joints.
Size Height at withers: 17–19 in.
Care Needs exercise and grooming; can cope with life in an apartment.
Character The Pinscher has been described as high-spirited and self-possessed. It is good natured and playful with children, and makes a fine guard.

Japanese Akita

The largest and best known of the Japanese breeds, the Akita originated in the Polar regions and has a history that can be traced back more than 300 years. It is swift, can work in deep snow, and is a strong swimmer.

Coat Outer coat coarse, straight, and stand-off; soft, dense undercoat.
Color Any, including white, brindle, and pinto, with or without mask.

Features Large, flat skull; broad forehead; small eyes and ears; long body; large, full tail.
Size Height at withers: dogs 26–28 in, bitches 24–26 in. Weight: 75–101 lb.
Care Requires daily brushing and exercise.
Character A versatile hunter and retriever, and a first-class guard dog, it is being kept widely as a pet. Can be formidable, needs obedience classes for its undoubted abilities.

Portuguese Water Dog

The Portuguese Water Dog is commonly found in the Algarve region of Portugal. It is a fisherman's dog, also a good rabbiter.

Coat Profuse and thick. Two types, both without undercoat: long and loosely waved; and shortish with compact curls.

Color Solid black, white, or brown; black and white, or brown and white; skin bluish.

Features Large, well-proportioned head; round eyes set well apart; heart-shape, dropped ears; wide, deep chest; tail thick at base.

Size Height at withers: dogs 19½–23 in, bitches 17–21 in. Weight: dogs 42–60 lb, bitches 35–50 lb.

Care Needs ample exercise and regular brushing and combing.

Character Intelligent and energetic, but obedient to its owner. A superlative swimmer and diver.

Swedish Vallhund

Closely resembling the Welsh Corgis, the Vallhund is a splendid cattle dog.

Coat Medium length, harsh, and close, with a soft, woolly undercoat.

Color Steel gray, grayish brown, grayish yellow, reddish yellow, or reddish brown; darker on back, neck, and sides; lighter on muzzle, throat, chest, belly, buttocks, feet, and hocks.

Features Head long; medium-size eyes; medium-size pointed ears; back level and well muscled; tail should not exceed 4 in, puppies may be docked by a veterinarian.

Size Height at withers: dogs 13–13¼ in, bitches 12–13 in. Weight: 25–35 lb.

Care Needs plenty of exercise.

Character A friendly, loyal, affectionate little dog, active and eager to please. Makes a good family pet.

Siberian Husky

Developed in ancient times by the
Chukchi people of north-east Asia as
a hardy sled dog with strength, speed,
and stamina, it became known for its
abilities after the gold rush. Huskies
became sled racing dogs, renowned
for search and rescue work.

Coat Medium in length, well-furred;
outer coat straight and smooth against body;
undercoat soft and dense.

Color All colors permissible; markings on
head common, including striking ones.

Features Medium-size head in
proportion to body; almond-shape eyes;
medium-size ears; arched neck; strong body
with a straight back; well-furred tail carried
gracefully, curled over back.

Size Height at withers: dogs 21–23½ in,
bitches 20–22 in. Weight: dogs 45–60 lb,
bitches 30–50 lb.

Care Needs plenty of space and exercise.

Character An intelligent and friendly
animal with considerable stamina. It is not
an aggressive dog and may be kept as a
family pet.

Alaskan Malamute

The Alaskan Malamute is a sociable member of the spitz family named after the Eskimo Mahlemut people. It has great stamina and speed, and is highly prized as a sled dog.

Coat Thick, coarse guard coat; dense, oily, woolly undercoat.

Color From light gray through intermediate shadings to black, or from gold through shades of red to liver; white on underbody, parts of legs, feet, and part of mask markings.

Features Broad, powerful head; almond-shape brown eyes; ears small in proportion to head, triangular; strong, powerful body; tail moderately high-set.

Size Height: dogs 25–28 in, bitches 23–26 in. Weight: 85–125 lb.

Care Needs a daily brushing and exercise.

Character Despite wolfish appearance, a gentle, kind-natured dog, a loyal and devoted companion, but is not good with other dogs.

Eskimo Dog

Developed to haul sleds in and around the Arctic Circle, the beautiful Eskimo Dog probably originated in eastern Siberia, and shared common ancestry with the Alaskan Malamute, Siberian Husky, and Samoyed.

Coat 6 in long, with a thick undercoat.
Color Any color, or combination of colors possible.

Features Well-proportioned head; dark brown or tawny eyes; short, firm ears set well apart; broad chest; large, bushy tail.
Size Height at shoulders: dogs 23–27 in, bitches 20–24 in. Weight: dogs 75–105 lb, bitches 60–90 lb.
Care Relishes vigorous outdoor exercise, and benefits from regular brushing.
Character An excellent sled dog of remarkable endurance and a fine guard, which rarely lives indoors with its owners.

Samoyed

The Samoyed, or Smiling Sammy, takes its name from the Siberian tribe of Samoyedes. This beautiful and devoted spitz variety has great powers of endurance and was one of the breeds used on expeditions to the North Pole. It has also been used as a guard and to hunt reindeer.

Coat Harsh, but not wiry, and straight, with thick, soft, short undercoat.
Color Pure white, white and biscuit, cream; outer coat silver-tipped.

Features Broad head; dark, almond-shape eyes; thick ears, slightly rounded at the tips; medium length back; long, profusely coated tail that is carried curled over the back.
Size Height at withers: dogs 21–23½ in, bitches 19–21 in. Weight: 50–65 lb.
Care Loves exercise; thick, water-resistant coat needs regular brushing and combing.
Character Living in the homes of its owners in its native land, the Sammy is a devoted dog, good with children, and obedient, if slightly independent.

HERDING DOGS

Newfoundland

Ponderous on land, the
Newfoundland is in its
element in water,
swimming strongly and
retrieving anything (or
anyone) in its path.

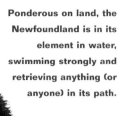

Probably descended from the Tibetan Mastiff, webbed feet and an oily coat allow the Newfoundland to remain in water for long periods of time. It aided fishermen and gained great fame as a life-saver, as valued in Newfoundland waters as the Saint Bernard is in the Swiss Alps.

Coat Flat, dense, and coarse-textured double coat; oily and water resistant. Outer coat moderately long, straight or slightly wavy.

Color Black, brown, gray, or Landseer (black head with black markings on a white ground).

Features Massive, broad head; small, dark brown eyes; small ears set well back; strong, broad, muscular body; thick tail.

Size Height at shoulders: dogs 28 in, bitches 26 in. Weight: dogs 130–150 lb, bitches 110–120 lb.

Care Needs a fair amount of space, regular exercise on hard ground, and daily brushing using a hard brush.

Character Rarely bad tempered unless provoked. Amazingly gentle with other breeds.

Bouvier des Flandres

Originating from the Flanders area, this shaggy dog was bred as a farm dog from a multiplicity of working breeds with the purpose of producing a good all-rounder. It was used in the hunt over rough ground, and as a herder, drover, protector, and guard.

Coat Rough, thick, and harsh with a soft dense undercoat.
Color From fawn to black, including brindle; white star on chest permissible.
Features Eyes alert in expression; ears set on high; broad, deep chest and short, strong body; tail usually docked to two or three joints.

Size Height at withers: dogs 24½–27½ in, bitches 23½–26½ in. Average weight: 88 lb.
Care Requires a good deal of exercise and regular brushing.
Character Can be rather fierce, but has a calm and sensible temperament. Intelligent, hardy, and trustworthy. Extremely loyal to its family and easily trained.

Traditionally the ears of the Bouvier des Flandres are clipped.

Hovawart

The name Hovawart comes from the German "Hofewart," meaning estate or watch dog, but its role is mainly that of a companion dog.

Coat Medium soft, fairly long, and close to the body.
Color Black and gold, blond and black.
Features Strong head, broad, convex forehead; ears triangular and set on high; body longer than height at withers, tail well feathered and carried low.
Size Height: dogs 24–27½ in, bitches 23–25½ in. Weight: dogs 66–88 lb, bitches about 55–77 lb.

Care Requires sufficient space and a firm hand in training.
Character An excellent guard dog, home-loving, fond of children, and easy to train. Will respond aggressively when provoked. Tends to be a one-man dog and is slow to mature. Requires a firm hand.

With its roots in the farmyard, the Hovawart is an excellent watchdog and good with children and stock.

German Shepherd Dog

The German Shepherd Dog, or Alsatian, is said to be a descendant of the Bronze Age wolf. The modern breed is perhaps the most widely recognized of all dogs, a versatile worker, that is renowned for its strength and agility.

Coat Medium length, straight, hard, and close-lying, with a dense, thick undercoat.
Color Solid black or gray; black saddle with tan or gold to light gray markings; gray with lighter or brown markings.
Features Strong head; medium-size eyes and ears; relatively long neck; long shoulder blades; straight back; strong hindquarters, broad and well muscled; long, bushy tail.

There is some color variation among German Shepherd Dogs, with the familiar sable background and black saddle being the most prevalent.

Size Height at shoulder: dogs 24–26 in, bitches 22–24 in. Weight: 75–95 lb.
Care Needs vigorous daily grooming, plenty of exercise, and, above all, a job to do.
Character Extremely intelligent and a first-class companion, obedience worker, and guard dog. Eminently trainable as police dog, in the armed services, guide dog for sight-impaired people, and in numerous other capacities.

Belgian Shepherd Dogs

All four varieties (Groenendael, Tervueren, Malinois, and the Laekenois) were developed from sheepdogs toward the end of the 19th century. The Groenendael is the most popular variety of Belgian Shepherd Dog.

Coat *Groenendael* and *Tervueren*: long, straight, and abundant, with an extremely dense undercoat. *Malinois:* very short on head, ears, lower legs, short on rest of body. *Laekenois:* harsh, wiry, and dry.

Color *Groenendael*: black; black with limited white; frosting (white or gray) on muzzle. *Tervueren*: all shades of red, fawn, gray, with black overlap. *Malinois*: all shades of red, fawn, gray, with black overlap. *Laekenois*: reddish fawn with black shading.

Features Finely chiseled head; medium-size eyes; ears distinctly triangular in appearance, stiff and erect; powerful but elegant body, broad-chested; medium-length tail, firmly set on and strong at the base.

Size Height: dogs 24–26 in, bitches 22–24 in. Weight: about 62 lb.

Care Needs plenty of exercise and regular grooming.

Character Intelligent and attentive, it works well in obedience trials and makes an excellent guard. Very protective, and can be kept in the home.

First to establish type among the motley of Belgian Shepherd Dogs was the Malinois.

The Groenendael is the most common and popular of the Belgian Shepherd Dogs.

The long-haired Tervueren, named after its region of origin, was developed by a local breeder.

The Laekenois is the rarest of the four breeds.

Briard

The best known of the French sheepdogs, the Briard is reputed to have come to Europe with Asian invaders before the end of the Middle Ages.

Coat Long and slightly wavy, and dry to the touch, with a fine, dense undercoat.
Color Solid black, or with white hairs; fawn; may have dark shading on ears, muzzle, back, and tail.

Features Strong, slightly rounded skull; dark eyes, set wide apart and horizontally placed; ears set on high; back firm and level; broad chest; long, well-feathered tail that has an upward hook at the tip.
Size Height at withers: dogs 23–27 in, bitches 22–25½ in. Weight: about 75 lb.
Care Takes pride in cleaning itself, but needs regular brushing. Requires plenty of exercise and space.
Character Makes a good family pet or farm dog. Good with children, intelligent, and fearless.

Picardy Shepherd

Also known as the Berger de Picard, this medium-size, shaggy, somewhat rustic-looking dog is said to be the oldest French herding dog and an unsurpassed worker with both sheep and cattle.

Coat Hard and moderate in length, with a heavy undercoat.
Color All shades of gray and fawn; white only in spot on chest and toes.

Features Large head with strong muzzle; dark eyes; ears carried erect; sturdy body; tail curved at the tip.
Size Height at withers: dogs 24–26 in, bitches 2 in less. Weight: 50–70 lb.
Care Requires plenty of space and exercise, and regular brushing.
Character Energetic and affectionate, it combines the role of working dog with that of family companion. Trustworthy with and devoted to children.

Australian Kelpie

Descended from short-haired, prick-eared collies imported from Scotland, the Kelpie is a superb working sheepdog, able to sustain itself without water for considerable periods of time.

Coat A close outer coat and short, dense undercoat.
Color Black, black and tan, red, red and tan, fawn, chocolate, and smoke blue, with or without tan.

Features Almond-shape eyes; prick ears; ribs well sprung; hindquarters show breadth and strength; tail hangs in slight curve.
Size Height at shoulders: about 20 in. Weight: about 30 lb.
Care Requires considerable exercise and vigorous daily brushing.
Character A fine sheepdog and a good, loyal companion.

Australian Cattle Dog

A superb worker which drives herds by nipping at the cattle's heels, the breed traces back to the now-extinct Black Bobtail.

Coat Smooth, hard, straight, and water-resistant top coat and short, normally dense undercoat.

Color Blue, blue mottled, or blue speckled with or without black, blue or tan markings on head; or red speckled with or without darker red markings on head.

Features Broad skull, slightly curved between the ears; alert, intelligent, oval-shape eyes; moderate-size to small ears; slightly long body; tail set low and follows slope of rump.

Size Height at withers: dogs 18–20 in, bitches 17–19 in. Weight: 35–45 lb.

Care Requires considerable exercise; benefits from a vigorous daily brushing.

Character Intelligent and good tempered, this superlative working dog is capable of covering immense distances.

Hungarian Puli

One of the best known of the Hungarian sheepdogs, the Puli is said to be a descendant of sheepdogs and over 1000 years old. It has herded sheep and, more recently, has been used for police work.

Coat Dense and weatherproof; outer coat wavy or curly, undercoat soft and woolly.
Color Black, rusty black, white, or various shades of gray and apricot, overall appearance of solid color.

Features Small, fine head with slightly domed skull; medium-size eyes; ears set slightly below top of skull; withers slightly higher than level of back; medium-length tail curling over loins.
Size Height at withers: dogs 16–17½ in, bitches 14½–16 in. Weight: dogs 28½–33 lb, bitches 22–28½ lb.
Care Requires a good amount of exercise and the cords of its coat have to be separated by hand, brushed, and combed.
Character A loyal, devoted, obedient, and intelligent dog, good with other pets, and slow to anger, it is reserved with humans outside its own family.

Anatolian Shepherd Dog

Large, powerful, and heavy-headed dogs, the Anatolian Shepherd Dog has lived in Turkey since Babylonian times (2800–1800 BC). Once used as war dogs, today they guard sheep.

Coat Short, dense, with a thick undercoat.
Color All colors acceptable, best is solid cream to fawn with black mask and ears.

Features Large, broad head, flat between the ears; small eyes; triangular ears rounded at the tips; deep chest; long tail.
Size Height at shoulders: dogs 29–32 in, bitches 28–31 in. Weight: dogs 110–141 lb, bitches 90½–130 lb.
Care Not suited to town life, and does not take kindly to strangers; requires considerable space and exercise, and should be brushed regularly.
Character A powerful, loyal, and loving dog, it is good with children, and makes a fine watchdog.

Maremma Sheepdog

The Maremma Sheepdog has two names in its native Italy because for centuries it spent the summer in the Abruzzi mountains, where there was good summer grazing, and the winter in the Maremma. It has never worked sheep like the Border Collie, but defended the flock against wolves and bears.

Coat Long, plentiful, and rather harsh; never curly.

Color All white.

Features Head conical in shape and appears large; bold eyes; ears small; strong, well-muscled body; tail set on low.

Size Height: dogs 25½–28½ in, bitches 23½–26½ in. Weight: dogs 77–99 lb, bitches about 66–88 lb.

Care Should be regularly groomed using a wire dog brush and, occasionally, a good cleansing powder.

Character A natural guard that will never forget a kindness or an injury.

An attractive and easily groomed pet, the Great Swiss Mountain Dog still enjoys a return to one of its traditional duties—pulling a cart or sled.

Great Swiss Mountain Dog

The largest of all Swiss mountain dogs, the Great Swiss is thought to descend from Molossus dogs, brought north by ancient Roman armies. An extremely robust dog with very strong hindquarters, it is capable of moving heavy loads and has also been used for search and rescue work in the mountains.

Coat Stiff and short.
Color Black with bright, symmetrical russet and white markings.

Features Flat, broad head; brown, medium-size eyes; triangular, medium-size ears; moderately long, strong, straight back; tail fairly heavy and reaching to the hocks.
Size Height: dogs 25½–27½ in, bitches 23½–25½ in.
Care Thrives in wide open spaces, and needs plenty of exercise; requires regular grooming with a bristle brush.
Character A faithful, gentle animal, generally devoted to children. It is alert and highly intelligent, and makes a fine watchdog, willing to protect its human family with its life.

Old English Sheepdog

The Old English Sheepdog, or Bobtail, has been developed through the crossing of the Briard with the Russian Owtcharka, which is related to the Hungarian sheepdogs. In the past it was used as a drover's dog and for defending flocks of sheep. In recent years the breed has enjoyed overwhelming popularity as a pet and show dog, owed in part to its frequent appearances in commercials.

Coat Profuse but not excessive, and a good harsh texture.

Color Any shade of gray, grizzle, or blue is acceptable.

Features Head in proportion to body; eyes set well apart; small ears carried flat to the side of the head; short, compact body; tail docked close to body.

Size Height at withers: dogs 22 in, bitches 21 in. Minimum weight: 66 lb.

Care Needs sufficient space and adequate amount of exercise.

Character A kindly dog of sound temperament, which gets on well with people, children, and other animals. Parents of young children who wanted a dog "like the one on television" have sometimes found the breed too much to handle because it is fairly large, heavy, and exuberant.

The Old English Sheepdog's tail is docked close to the body.

Grizzle is its typical coat color; gray and blue are also seen.

The Old English Sheepdog
makes a superb pet, but
needs a firm hand and
regular exercise.

Lancashire Heeler

A sporting dog and dispeller of
vermin, the Lancashire Heeler was
developed to herd cattle by nipping
at their heels, but it also has strong
terrier instincts and is an excellent
rabbiter and ratter.

Coat Short and smooth.
Color Black and tan, with rich tan
markings on muzzle, in spots on cheeks and
often above eyes, from knees downwards,
with desirable thumb-mark above feet,
inside legs, and under tail.
Features Richness of tan may fade with
age. White to be discouraged, except for a
very small white spot on forechest which is
permitted but not desirable.

Size Height at shoulders: dogs 12 in,
bitches 10 in. Average weight: 8–12 lb.
Care Requires an average amount of
exercise and daily brushing.
Character A happy, affectionate little
dog, which gets on well with humans and
other pets.

Shetland Sheepdog

The Shetland Sheepdog, or Sheltie, originated in the Shetland islands off the north coast of Scotland where it has bred true for more than 135 years.

Coat Outer coat of long, straight, harsh-textured hair; soft, short-haired, close undercoat.

Color Sable, tricolor, blue merle, black and white, and black and tan.

Features Refined head, with medium-size, almond-shape eyes, obliquely set; ears small and moderately wide at base; muscular, arched neck; back level; tail set low and tapering toward tip.

Size Height at withers: dogs about 14½ in, bitches about 14 in.

Care Requires daily grooming, using a stiff bristle brush and a comb; should not be kenneled outside.

Character An excellent choice of family pet; an intelligent, faithful dog which enjoys exercise, gets on well with children, and is generally obedient.

Welsh Corgi Pembroke

The Welsh Corgi Pembroke, a favorite of British royalty, has been a working dog since the 11th century—its job was to control the movement of cattle by nipping their heels. It may be descended from the Swedish Vallhund or from Flemish stock.

Coat Medium length and straight, with a dense undercoat; never soft, wavy, or wiry.

Color Red, sable, fawn, or black and tan, with or without white markings on legs, brisket, and neck; some white on head and foreface permissible.

Features Head foxy in shape and appearance; firm, upright ears with slightly rounded points; deep chest and moderately long body; short tail, may be docked if seen to be necessary.

Size Height at shoulders: about 10–12 in. Weight: dogs about 27 lb, bitches about 25 lb.

Care Puts on weight if underexercised. Coat needs daily brushing.

Character Extremely active and devoted little dogs.

Welsh Corgi Cardigan

The Welsh Corgi Cardigan has a similar history to the more popular Pembroke, and until the 1930s both Welsh Corgis were interbred. The Cardigan is heavier boned and larger bodied, and is easily distinguished from the Pembroke by its long, bushy, fox-like tail.

Coat Short or medium length, with a hard texture; short, thick undercoat.
Color Any, with or without white markings, but white should not predominate over other colors.

Features Head foxy in shape and appearance; medium-size eyes; upright ears; chest moderately broad with prominent breast bone; tail bushy, set in line with body.
Size Height at withers: 10½–12½ in. Weight: dogs 30–38 lb, bitches 25–34 lb.
Care Tendency to put on weight, so exercise regularly; water-resistant coat needs daily brushing.
Character Active and devoted. Said to have a slightly more equable temperament than the Pembroke.

Smooth Collie

The ancestors of both Rough and Smooth Collies were brought over from Iceland to Scotland over 400 years ago, where they were used as sheepdogs—the word "colley" is a Scottish term for a sheep with a black face and legs.

Coat Short, harsh, and smooth, with a dense undercoat.

Color Sable and white, tricolor, blue merle (the latter not in the UK).

Features Head should appear light in proportion to body; almond-shape eyes; ears small, and not too close together; body slightly long in relation to height; long tail usually carried low.

Size Height at shoulders: dogs 22–26 in, bitches 20–24 in. Weight: dogs 45–75 lb, bitches 40–65 lb.

Care Needs plenty of space and exercise. The coat is easier to groom than that of the Rough Collie.

Character Loyal, affectionate, easy to train; reliable with children; naturally suspicious of strangers and makes an excellent guard dog.

Rough Collie

The Rough Collie, sometimes called the Scots or Scottish Collie, is still best known as the star of the "Lassie" films. Identical to the Smooth Collie, apart from the length of its coat, the Rough Collie is much more common.

Coat Very dense, straight outer coat harsh to touch, with soft, furry, close undercoat.
Color Sable and white, tricolor, blue merle (not in UK shows).

Features Head should appear light in proportion to body; medium-size, almond-shape eyes; ears small and not too close together; body slightly long in relation to height; long tail.
Size Height at shoulders: dogs 22–25½ in, bitches 20–24 in. Weight: dogs 45–75 lb, bitches 40–65 lb.
Care Needs plenty of exercise and space but, despite the long coat, it is not difficult to groom.
Character Intelligent, hardy, has keen eyesight. Affectionate to its owners, it is easy to train and makes a good guard dog.

Bearded Collie

The Bearded Collie is believed to be one of the oldest herding dogs in Scotland. It is descended from purebred Polish Lowland Sheepdogs.

Coat Flat, harsh, and shaggy; can be slightly wavy but not curly; soft, furry, close undercoat.

Color Slate gray, reddish fawn, black, blue, all shades of gray, brown, or sandy, with or without white markings.

Features Broad, flat head; eyes toning with coat color; drooping ears; long body; tail set low, without a kink or twist.

Size Height at withers: dogs 21–22 in, bitches 20–21 in. Weight: 40–60 lb.

Care Enjoys plenty of exercise; requires daily brushing, very little combing, and the occasional bath.

Character The Beardie is an alert, self-confident, and active dog, good-natured and reliable with children. It makes a good pet.

Border Collie

The Border Collie is a descendant of working collies, bred for stamina and brains. It has the natural instinct to herd, and has excelled in sheepdog trials since 1873.

Coat Two varieties: moderately long, and smooth; both are thick and straight.
Color Variety of colors permissible; white should never predominate.
Features Oval-shape eyes set wide apart; ears set wide apart; body athletic in appearance; tail moderately long.

Size Height: dogs about 21 in, bitches slightly less. Weight: 30–45 lb.
Care Requires considerable exercise but only a regular groom with brush and comb.
Character Predominantly a working dog, it also excels at obedience competitions.

Appenzell Mountain Dog

The Appenzell takes its name from a canton in northern Switzerland. Used extensively at one time as a herding dog, and to haul carts of produce to market, it is still fairly common in its native land, but is today rarely seen in other countries.

Coat Short, dense, and hard.
Color Black and tan with white markings on head, chest, and feet; the tip of the tail is always white.

Features Head flat, broadest between ears; brown, rather small eyes; fairly small ears set on high; strong, straight back; medium-length, strong tail carried curled over the back.
Size Height: dogs 22–23 in, bitches 18½–20 in. Weight: 49–55 lb.
Care Needs plenty of food and exercise, and a daily brushing.
Character A resilient, intelligent dog that is easily trained, the adaptable Appenzell makes an excellent farm and rescue dog, companion, and guard.

Norwegian Buhund

The Norwegian Buhund is a spitz type, and bears a strong resemblance to the Iceland Dog. In Norway, it is used as a guard and farm dog, for herding cattle, sheep, and ponies, and is one of that country's national dogs.

Coat Close, harsh, and smooth, with a soft woolly undercoat.
Color Wheaten, black, red, or wolf-sable; small symmetrical white markings permissible; black mask.

Features Light head, broad between the ears; ears set on high; strong, short body; short, thick tail set high and carried tightly curled over back.
Size Height: dogs about 17–18 in, bitches smaller. Weight: 26–40 lb.
Care Needs a fair amount of exercise, and daily brushing and combing.
Character A natural herder, it is a gentle, friendly dog, and a reliable playmate for children.

GUNDOGS

Chesapeake Bay Retriever

The Chesapeake Bay Retriever probably descended from a Newfoundland which mated with various working breeds in the Chesapeake Bay area. Combining the superb swimming ability of the Newfoundland and the duck-retrieving abilities of local dogs, the Chesapeake Bay Retriever was kept strictly as a sporting dog until fairly recently. However, it is now finding its way into the family home and the show ring.

Coat A distinctive feature: thick and reasonably short (not over 1½ in long), with harsh, oily outercoat and dense, fine, woolly undercoat.

Color Dead grass (straw to bracken), sedge (red-gold), or any shade of brown; white spots (the smaller the better) on chest, toes, and belly permissible.

Features Broad, round head; medium-size eyes; small ears; strong, deep, broad chest; tail should extend to hock.

Size Height: dogs 23–26 in, bitches 21–24 in. Weight: dogs 65–80 lb, bitches 55–70 lb.

Care Oily coat needs regular brushing and gives off a slight odor. Needs plenty of exercise and does best if it has sufficient space to roam freely.

Character The Chesapeake is a good natured pet, and does well in field trials.

The reddish-brown coat of this
Chesapeake Bay Retriever clearly
shows the typical waviness on the
neck, back, and loins.

Nova Scotia Duck Tolling Retriever

This breed originated in the Maritime Provinces of Canada, and is believed to be of Chesapeake Bay and Golden Retriever stock. Well boned down to its strong webbed feet, its job in life is to thrash about at the water's edge in order to attract the attention of wildfowl, a performance that has become known as tolling.

Coat Moderately long and close lying, with a thick, wavy undercoat.
Color Red fox, with white marking on chest, feet, and tip of tail, and sometimes on face.

Features Broad head with well-defined stop; webbed feet.
Size Height at shoulders: 17–21 in. Weight: about 37–51 lb.
Care Needs plenty of exercise, and regular grooming with a bristle brush and comb.
Character Quiet and easy to train; makes a good family pet.

Curly-coated Retriever

Probably descended from the Irish Water Spaniel or the Standard Poodle, the Curly-coated was one of the first breeds to be used seriously for retrieving purposes in England, but is now rarely seen outside the show ring.

Coat A mass of crisp, small curls all over, except on face.

Color Black or liver.

Features Long, well-proportioned head; black or dark brown eyes; small ears, set on low; muscular shoulders and deep chest; moderately short tail.

Size Height at withers: dogs about 27 in, bitches about 25 in. Weight: 70–80 lb.

Care Requires vigorous exercise, best in a country environment. Its curly coat only needs to be dampened down and massaged with circular movements.

Character A better guard than other retrievers, and a reliable family dog.

Flat-coated Retriever

Once known as the Wavy-coated Retriever, the Flat-coat is generally thought to have evolved from the Labrador Retriever and spaniels. It is superlative at picking up game, and an excellent wildfowler and water dog.

Coat Dense, fine to medium texture, medium length and lying flat.

Color Solid black or solid liver.

Features Long, clean head; medium-size eyes; small ears well set on, lying close to side of head; deep chest and strong body; tail short, straight, and well set on.

Size Height: dogs 23–24 in, bitches 22–23 in. Weight: dogs 60–80 lb, bitches about 55–70 lb.

Care Needs plenty of exercise and also a daily brushing.

Character Intelligent, with a kindly temperament; hardy and may be kept in outside kennels.

Labrador Retriever

The Labrador Retriever arrived in Britain in the 1830s with Newfoundland fishermen who used the dogs to help them land their nets. One of the most popular dogs, it is a first-class gundog, a fine swimmer, and also works as a guide dog for sight-impaired people.

Coat Short and dense, without wave or feathering; weather-resistant undercoat.
Color Wholly black, yellow, or liver/chocolate; yellows range from light cream to red fox; small white spot on the chest is permissible.

Features Head broad with defined stop; medium-size eyes; ears not large or heavy; chest of good width and depth; distinctive "otter" tail.
Size Shoulder height: dogs 22½–24½ in, bitches 21½–23½ in. Weight: dogs 60–75 lb, bitches 55–70 lb.
Care Needs plenty of exercise and regular brushing. It can be kept indoors as a family pet or in an outdoor kennel.
Character Exuberant, but easy to train, the Labrador is good with children.

Golden Retriever

According to a story the Golden Retriever originates from a troupe of eight Russian sheepdogs, performing in a circus. Whatever the truth, it is an excellent family dog with a kind, brown eye.

Coat Flat or wavy with good feathering; dense, water-resistant undercoat.
Color Any shade of gold or cream, but neither red nor mahogany; a few white hairs on chest are permissible.

Features Head balanced and well-chiseled; dark brown eyes; moderate-size ears; deep chest and well balanced body; tail set on and carried level with back.
Size Height at withers: dogs 22–24 in, bitches 20–22 in. Weight: dogs 65–75 lb, bitches 55–65 lb.
Care It requires regular brushing and ample exercise, and is best suited to a country environment; will adapt to suburban conditions provided that good walks and a garden are available.
Character The Golden Retriever is an ideal sportman's companion, family pet, an excellent gundog, and gentle with children. This beautiful animal also makes a popular show dog.

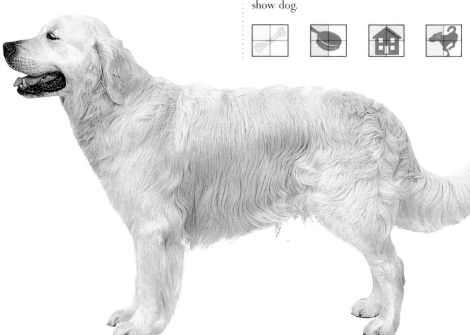

English Springer Spaniel

The English Springer is one of the oldest of the British spaniels. It was originally used for flushing or "springing" game from cover before shotguns were in use.

Coat Close, straight, and weather-resistant; never coarse.

Color Liver and white, black and white; either of these with tan markings.

Features Medium-length skull; medium-size eyes; long, wide ears; strong body; tail set low, and never carried above the level of the back.

Size Shoulder height: dogs 20 in, bitches 19 in. Weight: 49–55 lb.

Care Needs plenty of exercise, a daily brushing, and regular checks to ensure that mud does not become lodged in its paws or its ears. May not be a good choice for the houseproud because it tends to have a good shake when it comes in out of the rain!

Character An intelligent, loyal, and popular gundog, which also makes a reliable family pet and is generally good with children.

Welsh Springer Spaniel

The Welsh Springer Spaniel, or its forerunner, is mentioned in the earliest records of the Laws of Wales, which date back to about AD 1300. It is possible that these red and white spaniels are a cross between the English Springer and the Clumber.

Coat Straight and flat, silky in texture; some feathering on chest, underside of body, and legs.

Color Rich red and white only.

Features Slightly domed head; medium-size, hazel or dark eyes; ears set moderately low; strong, muscular body; tail well set on and low.

Size Height at withers: dogs 18–19 in, bitches 17–18 in. Weight: 35–45 lb.

Care Needs brushing daily, checks for mud in its paws or ears, and plenty of exercise.

Character Loyal and hard-working, it is a good swimmer, has an excellent nose, and combines the role of family dog and sportsman's companion.

Field Spaniel

The Field Spaniel has the same origin as the Cocker Spaniel, being, in effect, a larger version of it. It was bred to produce an exaggeratedly long body and short legs.

Coat Long, flat, and glossy, without curls; silky in texture.

Color Black, liver, or roan with tan markings; clear black, white, or liver and white unacceptable.

Features Head conveys high breeding, character, and nobility; eyes wide open; moderately long and wide ears; deep chest; tail set low and docked.

Size Height at withers: dogs 18 in, bitches 17 in. Weight: 35–55 lb.

Care Thrives on plenty of exercise; needs to be brushed and combed every day, taking care that its coat does not become matted.

Character Possessing an equable temperament, it makes a good household pet and gundog.

English Cocker Spaniel

The smallest in the gundog group, the Cocker Spaniel is also called the Merry Cocker because of its wagging tail. It originated in Spain (the word "spaniel" comes from *Espagnol*, meaning Spanish). Spaniels have been known since the 14th century and were used in falconry.

Coat Flat and silky in texture.
Color Various; self (pure) colors, no white allowed on chest.
Features Square muzzle; eyes full but not prominent; strong, compact body; tail set on slightly lower than line of back.
Size Height: dogs 15½–17 in, bitches 15–16 in. Weight: 28–32 lb.
Care Needs careful brushing and combing every day, and immense care must be taken to dislodge any mud that may have become caked in its paws or its ears.
Character A gentle and popular pet, as well as a first-class gundog, able both to flush out and retrieve.

Excellent in the field,
the English Cocker
tends to work close
to the guns.

Sussex Spaniel

One of the rarest of spaniels, the Sussex Spaniel has been known in southern England for 200 years. It is used mainly for partridge and pheasant, being too small to take a hare. It works in thick cover, giving tongue (barking) as it works so that its handler knows where it is.

Coat Abundant and flat, ample weather-resistant undercoat.

Color Rich golden liver, shading to golden at tips of hairs, gold predominating; dark liver or puce is undesirable.

Features Wide head, slightly rounded between the ears; fairly large, hazel-colored eyes with a soft expression; fairly large, thick ears; deep, well-developed chest; tail set on low and never carried above level of back.

Size Height at withers: 13–16 in. Weight: 35–50 lb.

Care Requires a daily brush and comb, and care must be taken that mud does not become caked in its ears and feet.

Character A working spaniel with an excellent nose, an ideal country dog; attaches itself to one person; loyal and easy to train.

Irish Water Spaniel

Evidence for water dogs and water spaniels goes back to AD 17 and some form of water spaniel has been known in Ireland for more than 1000 years. The Irish Water Spaniel, the tallest of the spaniels, is thought to have been developed through crosses with Poodles and Curly-coated Retrievers. Before 1859, there were two separate strains of the breed in Ireland, one in the north and one in the south. It would seem that the southern strain, which resembled the Standard Poodle, formed the basis of the modern breed.

Coat Dense, tight ringlets on neck, body, and top part of tail; longer, curling hair on legs and topknot; face, rear of tail, and back of legs below hocks smooth.

Color Rich, dark liver.

Features Good-sized, high-domed head; small, almond-shape eyes; long, oval-shape ears; arching neck; deep chest; short tail.

Size Height: dogs 21–24 in, bitches 20–23 in. Weight: dogs 55–65lb, bitches 45–58lb.

Care Needs to be groomed at least once a week with a steel comb. Some stripping of unwanted hair and trimming round feet is usually necessary.

Character Brave, loving, and intelligent. Has a fine nose, and will work and quarter as a spaniel. A strong swimmer that is large enough to retrieve large or injured wild fowl, such as geese, from deep water.

American Cocker Spaniel

The name of the American Cocker Spaniel is derived from the predilection of the English Cockers for "cocking," or hunting woodcock. Distinguished by its small stature—suited to the lighter New World game birds—shorter head and extremely dense coat, it is the smallest of American gundogs.

Coat Short and fine on head, medium length on body, with enough undercoat to give protection.

Color Black, jet black; black and tan and brown and tan, with definite tan markings on jet black or brown body; particolors and tricolors.

Features Head rounded and well developed; eyes full and looking directly forward; back slopes slightly downward from shoulders to tail; the tail is characteristically docked.

Size Height: dogs 14½–15½ in, bitches 13½–14½ in. Weight: 24–28 lb.

Care Needs plenty of exercise, daily brushing and combing.

Character A useful, all-purpose gundog, makes a fine housepet, and it is usually good with children.

Careful attention is needed to the American Cocker Spaniel's long, silky coat.

American Cocker Spaniel ranks among top dog breeds in the United States.

Clumber Spaniel

The Clumber is the heaviest of the
spaniels, with the Basset and the now
extinct Alpine Spaniel in its ancestry.
A favorite of several generations of
the British royal family, the Clumber
is slower than lighter-boned dogs in
the field, but is nevertheless a good,
steady gundog, excelling in flushing
out game and as a retriever.

Coat Abundant, close, and silky.
Color Plain white body with lemon
markings preferred for show dogs, though
orange is allowed. Slight head markings and
freckled muzzle.
Features Massive, square, medium-length
head; clean, dark-amber eyes, slightly
sunken; large, vine-leaf shape ears; long,
heavy body close to ground; chest deep; tail
set low and feathered.
Size Height at withers: dogs 19–20 in,
bitches 17–19 in. Weight: dogs 70–84 lb,
bitches 55–70 lb.
Care Needs a fair amount of brushing, and
care must be taken that mud does not
become lodged between its toes.
Character Good temperament and may
be kept as a pet, but ideally it should be a
working gundog.

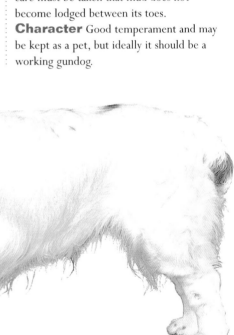

English Setter

The oldest and most distinctive of the four breeds of setter—which sit or "set" when they find prey— the English Setter has been known since the 14th century.

Coat Short, straight, and dense.
Color Black and white (blue belton), orange and white (orange belton), lemon and white (lemon belton), liver and white (liver belton), or tricolor (blue belton and tan or liver belton and tan); those without heavy patches of color but flecked (belton) all over are preferred.
Features Head lean and noble; eyes neither deep nor prominent; ears moderately low set; back short, level, and well muscled; high withers; tail set on almost in line with back, scimitar shape but not turning upward, soft feathering.

Size Height: dogs 25–27 in, bitches 24–25 in. Weight: 40–70 lb.
Care Needs daily brushing with a stiff brush and the use of a steel comb.
Character Strikingly beautiful, loyal, and affectionate, it combines the role of family pet and sportman's dog. It is good with children, can live as one of the family or be kenneled out of doors.

Gordon Setter

Scotland's only gundog, the Gordon was bred in the late 1770s from Bloodhound and Collie. Gordons are not so fast or stylish as other setters.

Coat Short and fine on head, fronts of legs, and tips of ears; moderately long over rest of body, flat and free from curl.

Color Deep, shining coal black, without rustiness, and with lustrous tan (chestnut red) markings; black pencilling on toes, and black streak under jaw permissible.

Features Head deep rather than broad; dark brown eyes; medium-size ears; body of moderate length; tail straight or slightly curved, not too long.

Size Height at shoulders: dogs 24–27 in, bitches 23–26 in. Weight: dogs 55–80 lb, bitches 45–70 lb.

Care Needs plenty of space and lots of exercise, and not best suited to town life.

Character A tireless worker, able to withstand heat better than other setters. Good as gundog as well as family pet, and a better watchdog than other setters.

Irish Setter

The Irish Setter, or Red Setter, was developed by crossing Irish Water Spaniels, Spanish Pointers, and the English and Gordon Setters. Although it originated in Ireland, the breed came into its own in Victorian England, where its speed and energy made it ideal as a gundog working in large, open expanses of countryside.

Coat Short and fine on head, fronts of legs, and tips of ears; moderately long, free, and as straight as possible on rest of body with good feathering.

Color Rich chestnut with no trace of black; white markings on chest, throat, chin, or toes, or small star on forehead, or narrow streak or blaze on nose or face are allowed when showing.

Features Long, lean head; dark hazel to dark brown eyes; moderate-size ears; deep chest, rather narrow in front; tail moderate in length in relation to body.

Size Height: 25–27 in. Weight: 60–70 lb.

Care Requires plenty of exercise as well as daily brushing.

Character Very good-natured and loving with boundless energy. Has particular affinity with horses, but does not make a good guard dog.

Irish Red and White Setter

The Irish Red and White Setter evolved from spaniels, probably red and white spaniels, that were brought to Ireland from France and crossed with pointers.

Coat Flat, straight, and finely textured with good feathering.

Color Clearly particolored with pearl white base and solid red patches; mottling and flecking, but not roaning, permitted around face and feet, and up foreleg to elbow and up hind leg as far as hock.

Features Head broad in proportion to body; hazel or dark brown eyes; ears set level with eyes; body strong and muscular; tail strong at root and tapering to fine point.

Size Height: 23½–27 in. Weight: 40–70 lb.

Care Needs space and plenty of exercise; requires daily brushing.

Character Happy, good-natured and affectionate, a sportsman's dog and family pet.

Saint Germain Setter

A refined and stylish dog, the Saint Germain Setter is said to have derived from a 19th century mating between an English Pointer and a French Setter. It is an attractive gundog, resembling the English Pointer, but not as heavily boned.

Coat Short and soft.
Color White with orange markings.
Features Fairly broad head; large, well-set, golden-brown eyes; ears set on level with eyes; short, straight back; loins strong, short, and slightly arched; tail undocked.
Size Height: dogs 20–25 in, bitches 21–23 in. Weight: 40–57 lb.
Care Needs a brush and rub down every few days, and requires plenty of exercise.
Character A strong hunting dog, but with less refinement and sense of smell than the English Pointer. May be used against large game, and also hunts pheasants and rabbit. It has a good gallop. Affectionate, gentle, and intelligent, but can be stubborn.

Bourbonnais Setter

Although associated with central France, the Bourbonnais Setter seems to derive from the Pyrenees. Its ancestors gradually spread out to other regions, and crossings with local dogs produced varieties which took the name of their new home. The Bourbonnais, often described as the short-tailed setter because it is born without a tail, has a striking Dalmatian-like coat pattern on a distinctly thickset body.

Coat Short.

Color White and light brown; fawn without large markings, but having small spots fused into the white, distributed uniformly over the body.

Features Very long head with arched skull and slight stop; large, dark amber eyes, not sunken; long ears reaching to throat; broad, slightly convex back, tail very short and set low.

Size Average height: 21 in. Weight: 40–57 lb.

Care Requires a fair amount of exercise, and needs a brush and rub down every few days.

Character A good-natured sporting and family dog; easy to train.

Pointer

The Pointer is famed for its classic stance, pointing with nose and tail in the direction of game. Popular around the world, it is thought to have originated in Spain or England, through crossings of Foxhound, Bloodhound, and Greyhound.

Coat Short, dense, and smooth.

Color Lemon and white, orange and white, liver and white, black and white; self (pure) colors and tricolors also correct.

Features Medium-width head with pronounced stop; dark, round, intense eyes; ears set on level with eyes; thin, sloping shoulders; deep chest; tail thicker at root, tapering to a point.

Size Height at withers: dogs 25–28 in, bitches 23–26 in. Weight: dogs 55–75 lb, bitches 45–65 lb.

Care Needs regular brushing, plenty of exercise, and is not suited to town life.

Character Sportman's companion and family pet; affectionate, obedient, easy to train, and good with children.

German Pointer

The German Short-haired Pointer is of Spanish origin and was probably derived from crossing the Spanish Pointer with a scenthound, thereby producing a dog that would both point and trail. English Foxhound blood is also believed to have been added. The breed was developed in Germany about 100 years ago.

Coat *Short-haired* Short and flat; coarse to the touch. *Wire-haired* Thick and harsh, with dense undercoat.

Color *Short-haired* Solid liver, liver and white spotted, liver and white spotted and ticked; liver and white ticked; the same variations with black instead of liver; not tricolor. *Wire-haired* Liver and white, solid liver, also black and white; solid black and tricolor undesirable in show dogs.

Features *Short-haired* Broad, clean-cut head, with slightly molded crown; medium-size eyes; broad ears set on high; chest should appear deep rather than wide, but in proportion to body; tail starts high and thick, growing gradually thinner toward tip. *Wire-haired* Broad head balanced in proportion to body; slightly rounded crown; medium-size, oval eyes; ears medium-size in relation to head: chest should appear deep rather than wide but not out of proportion to rest of body; tail starts high and thick, growing gradually thinner toward tip.

Size *Short-haired*—height at withers: dogs 23–25 in, bitches 21–23 in. Weight: dogs

55–71 lb, bitches 44–60 lb. *Wire-haired*—height at shoulders: dogs 24–25 in, bitches 22–24 in. Weight: dogs 55–75 lb, bitches 44–64 lb.

Care Neither breed of Pointer requires a lot of grooming. The wire-haired breed is less suitable as a household pet. Both types of dog require plenty of regular exercise and adequate space.

Except for its bristly coat, the German Wire-haired Pointer (right) is very similar to the Short-haired, which contributed to its make-up.

Character Both varieties are powerful, strong, and versatile hunting dogs, equally at home on land or in the water. Short-haired is easy to train and good with children. Wire-haired Pointer is an active, responsive dog, but it has some aggressive qualities.

Large and Small Münsterländers

Officially recorded as one of the newest pointing and retrieving gundog breeds, the Large Münsterländer has been established in its native Germany as an all-purpose gundog since the beginning of the 18th century.

Coat Moderately long and dense, with feathering.

Color *Large* Head solid black, white blaze, strip or star allowed; body white or blue roan with black patches, flecks, ticks in any combination. *Small* Liver and white with ticking.

Features Head well proportioned in relation to body and slightly elongated; medium-size, intelligent eyes; broad, high-set ears; strong back; tail well set on in line with back.

Size *Large* Height: dogs 24 in, bitches 23 in. Weight: dogs 55–65 lb, bitches 55 lb. *Small* Height: 19–22 in. Weight: 33 lb.

Care Need plenty of exercise and at least daily brushing.

Character Loyal, affectionate, and trustworthy dogs, sportsmen's companions, as well as family pets.

Hungarian Vizsla

The Hungarian Vizsla, or Magyar Vizsla, is the national hunting dog of Hungary. The Hungarian word *vizsla* means "responsive" or "alert." This smooth-haired setter was bred for the temperature extremes of the central Hungarian plain (Puszta). It is likely that the German Weimaraner, to which it bears a strong resemblance, and Transylvanian pointing dogs played a part in its early development. There is a wire-haired form of the Vizsla, rarer than the smooth-haired variety, which is favored in its native Hungary for working in water. It was not until after the Second World War that the Vizsla became widely known.

Coat Short, dense, and straight; tightly fitting.
Color Russet gold; small white marks on chest and feet are acceptable.
Features Lean, elegant head with a long muzzle; long, thin ears, set moderately low; short, level, well-muscled back; deep chest with prominent breastbone; tail moderately thick, set low, and docked.
Size Height at withers: dogs 22½–25 in, bitches 21–24 in. Weight: 44–66 lb.

Care Needs plenty of exercise and the coat should be brushed regularly.
Character A versatile, easily trained gundog, adept at hunting, pointing, and retrieving, and bred for temperature extremes. It is gentle and responsive, is good with children, and makes a first-class pet.

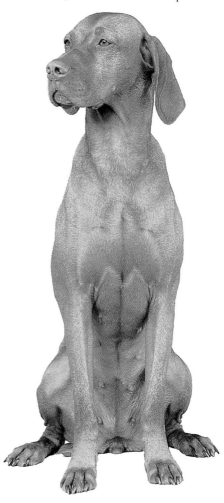

Italian Spinone

The Italian Spinone is an ancient
gundog breed. It has also recently
become a contender in the
international show ring and in field
trials. Opinions about the dog's
origins vary, as to whether it is of
setter descent, a relative of the
coarse-haired Italian Segugio, or a
Griffon cross. Yet others believe this
powerful, versatile hunter originated
in France, later finding its way to
Piedmont in Italy, and that its
evolution is attributable to the French
Griffon, German Pointers, the
Porcelaine, the Barbet, and the
Korthals Griffon.

Coat Rough, thick, fairly wiry with a
dense undercoat.
Color White, white with orange
markings, solid white peppered orange,
white with brown markings, white speckled
with brown (brown roan), with or without
brown markings.
Features Expressive eyes, varying in
color from yellow to ocher; long, triangular
ears; sturdy back, body length equal to
height at withers; tail thick at base and
carried horizontally.
Size Height at shoulders: dogs 23–27 in,
bitches 23–25 in. Weight: dogs 70–82 lb,
bitches 62–70 lb.

Care Needs plenty of vigorous exercise, is
a fine swimmer, and is best suited to the
freedom of country life.
Character Affectionate, agreeable, and of
loyal temperament. Will point and has a soft
mouth for retrieving game undamaged.

Brittany

The Brittany is the only spaniel in the world that points to game. It may be the progeny of an Irish Red and White Setter dog and a Breton bitch.

Coat Body coat flat and dense, never curly; a little feathering on legs.
Color Orange and white or liver and white in clear or roan patterns, or tricolor.

Features Rounded, medium-length head; expressive eyes; drop ears; deep chest reaching to the level of the elbows; tail naturally short or usually docked to 4in, with a small twist of hair on the end, carried level with back.
Size Height at shoulders: 17½–20½in. Weight: 30–40 lb.
Care Requires daily brushing and plenty of exercise.
Character Has an excellent nose and needs gentle handling.

Kooikerhondje

A fairly old breed, native to the
Netherlands, the Kooikerhondje had
to draw ducks out of their cover by
the banks of a dyke that was covered
with netting. When the ducks
investigated, the dyke was closed.

Coat Moderately long and slightly wavy;
feathering on chest, legs, and tail.
Color Clear white with red patches.
Features Head broad, with long
hair on ears, pointed nose; tail long
and curled to one side, bushy.
Size Height at shoulders: 15 in. Weight:
20–24 lb.
Care Needs plenty of exercise and
regular brushing.
Character Intelligent, affectionate, and
lively; good companion and a handy size for a
household pet.

Weimaraner

The Weimaraner or "Silver Ghost" is said to have been purpose-bred as a gundog in the 19th century by the Grand Duke Karl August of Weimar. A fine gundog, it was originally used against big game and, in more recent times, has worked as a police dog.

Coat Short, smooth, and sleek.

Color Preferably silver gray; shades of mouse or roe gray permissible.

Features Head moderately long and aristocratic; medium-size eyes; long ears; deep chest and moderately long body; tail characteristically docked.

Size Height at withers: dogs 24–27 in, bitches 22–25 in. Weight: 70–85 lb.

Care Best housed indoors; requires only little grooming.

Character Good natured and distinctive looking, with a metallic silver-gray coat and amber or blue-gray eyes. Obedient and agile, it makes a fine pet provided that it has an outlet for its keen intelligence.

HOUNDS

Greyhound

The Greyhound is arguably the purest breed on Earth, appearing to have changed little from dogs depicted on the tombs of Egyptian pharaohs. It is also mentioned in the Holy Bible in the Book of Solomon. It is likely that the Greyhound was brought by Celts to Britain, where it became a favorite with nobility in the 11th and 14th centuries. Possessing keen eyesight and capable of great speed, this sighthound was highly valued as a courser and, more recently, as a competitor on the racing track.

Coat Fine and close.
Color Black, white, red, blue, fawn, fallow brindle, or any of these colors broken with white.
Features Long, moderately broad head; bright, intelligent eyes: small, close-shape ears; long, elegant neck; deep, capacious chest; long tail set on rather low.
Size Height: dogs 28–30 in, bitches 28 in. Weight: dogs 65–70 lb, bitches 60–65 lb.
Care Needs a daily brush and regular exercise on hard ground; it takes up relatively little space, having a liking for its own special corner.
Character Gentle, faithful, good with children, the Greyhound chases anything that moves.

Reputedly the fastest
dog on earth, the
Greyhound has
fanciers dating back
to the Egyptian
Fourth Dynasty.

American Foxhound

A highly valued hunting dog, the American Foxhound is a descendant of English Foxhounds taken to Maryland, United States, in 1650. George Washington is also known to have imported Foxhounds from England.

Coat Hard and close.

Color All colors acceptable.

Features Large skull; large, broad, pendant, wide-set ears, flat to head; streamlined body: saber-shaped tail.

Size Height: dogs 22–25 in, bitches 21–24 in.

Care Needs a large amount of exercise; needs only an occasional sponge over before a hound show.

Character Good natured, can become less attentive and more wilful as it grows older.

English Foxhound

The English Foxhound is a descendant of the heavier Saint Hubert Hounds and another extinct hound, the Talbot. The Foxhound's prime function is to hunt foxes alongside mounted huntsmen. It can work for several hours without a break in various types of terrain.

Coat Short and hard.

Color Tricolor—black, white, and tan—or bicolor with a white background.

Features Head not heavy, and with pronounced brow; ears set on low and hanging close to head; muscular, level back; straight legs; tail (stern) well set on and carried gaily.

Size Height: dogs 22–25 in, bitches 21–24 in. Weight: 65–70 lb.

Care and Character Strong, lively, and noisy; never kept as pets, property of individual hunting packs.

Otterhound

The strongly built British Otterhound probably evolved from foxhounds and other hunting dogs.

Coat Long, about 2 in, dense, rough, and harsh, but not wiry.
Color All hound colors.

Features Clean, very imposing head; intelligent eyes; long, pendulous ears—a unique feature of the breed—set on level with corner of eyes; deep chest with fairly deep well-sprung rib-cage; tail (stern) set on high, carried up when alert or moving.
Size Height: dogs 24–27 in, bitches 23–26 in. Weight: dogs 75–115 lb, bitches 66–100 lb.
Care Can be kenneled outdoors, though many Otterhounds do live indoors. Needs a lot of exercise. Its rough coat should be groomed once a week, and the dog needs to be bathed as necessary.
Character Amiable, but stubborn. Can be somewhat destructive within the household if undisciplined.

Bloodhound

The Bloodhound, or Chien de Saint Hubert, is one of the oldest hound breeds. It is generally believed that the earliest ancestors of the Bloodhound were bred in Mesopotamia in 2,000–1,000 BC. The Bloodhound has the keenest sense of smell of any domestic animal. Able to follow a days-old scent, it has been used to track down lost people as well as game. Having found its quarry, this gentle animal does not kill it.

Coat Smooth, short, and weatherproof.

Color Black and tan, liver (red) and tan, or red.

Features Head narrow in proportion to length, and long in proportion to body; medium-size eyes; thin, soft ears set very low; well-sprung ribs; tail (stern) long, thick, and tapering to a point.

Size Height: dogs 25–27 in, bitches 23–25 in. Weight: dogs 90–110 lb, bitches 80–100 lb.

Care Needs adequate exercise; best suited to a rural environment. It should be groomed daily with a hound glove.

Character Good with children and exceedingly affectionate; an ideal companion for those with space and energy, and tolerant neighbors who do not object to its baying.

Long, drooping ears, wrinkles, and dewlaps give the Bloodhound an expression of inconsolable sadness.

Basset Hound

The Basset Hound was bred from the French Basset Artésien Normand, crossed with the Bloodhound to produce a slow but sure dog, which was used in tracking rabbits and hare. With its Bloodhound expression and short legs, the Basset is among the few hound breeds to have become popular household pets.

Coat Hard, smooth, short, and dense.
Color Generally black, white, and tan (tricolor) or lemon and white (bicolor), but any recognized hound color acceptable.

Features Head domed, with some stop and occipital bone prominent; lozenge-shape eyes; ears set low; body long, and deep throughout length; tail (stern) well set on.
Size Height at withers: 13–14 in. Weight: 40–60 lb.
Care Needs lots of exercise. Has a propensity to wander, and fencing is essential. Requires daily grooming with a hound glove.
Character Mainly kept as a companion and pet. A lovable animal, gets on well with children.

Beagle

This small hound has existed in Britain at least since the reign of King Henry VIII (1509–47). His daughter Elizabeth I of England (1533–1603) kept numerous Beagles, some of which were so small they could be put in a pocket and so became known as Pocket Beagles (now extinct). The breed is often known as the "singing Beagle," but it is not usually noisy indoors, reserving its voice for the chase.

Coat Short, dense, and weatherproof.

Color Any recognized bound color other than liver; tip of stern, white.

Features Head fairly long and powerful without being coarse; dark brown or hazel eyes; long ears with pointed tips; top-line straight and level; sturdy tail.

Size Height: two varieties: under 13 in, and 13–15 in.

Care Short, weatherproof coat requires little attention; needs average exercise when kept as a pet.

Character Affectionate, determined, and healthy; long-lived and good with children. It makes a good family pet but is not renowned for obedience.

Dachshund

There are six varieties of Dachshund, which is also known as the Teckel or Badger Hound. They are the Smooth-haired, the Long-haired, and the Wire-haired, each occurring as both Standard and Miniature. The Dachshund derives from the oldest breeds of German hunting dogs, such as the Bibarhund, and is known to have existed as long ago as the 16th century. Originally there was only one variety, the Smooth-haired Dachshund, whose wrinkled paws are a characteristic now rarely seen. The Wire-haired was produced through the introduction of Dandie Dinmont and other terrier blood, while the Long-haired was formed by introducing the German Stöber, a gundog, to a Smooth-haired Dachshund and Spaniel cross.

Coat *Smooth-haired* Dense, short, and smooth. *Long-haired* Soft and straight, and only slightly wavy. *Wire-haired* Short, straight, and harsh, with a long undercoat.

Color All colors but white permissible when showing; small patch on chest permitted but not desirable; dappled dogs may include white but should be evenly marked all over.

Features Long head, conical in appearance when seen from above; medium-size eyes; ears set on high; body long and full-muscled; tail continues along line of spine but is slightly curved.

Size Height: 5–9 in. Weight:
> *Standard* 15–33 lb
> *Miniature* 11 lb.

Care Short-haired needs only daily grooming with a hound glove and soft cloth. Wire-haired and Long-haired should be brushed and combed. Dachshunds are prone to back problems and should not jump up to or from heights.

Character Active and devoted. Makes a good family pet and watchdog—it has a loud bark for its size.

Smooth-haired Dachshund

Whippet

The Whippet, which looks like a Greyhound in miniature, is the fastest breed in the world: it has been timed at 8.4 seconds over a standard 150 yd straight course (36.52 mph). Known as the "poor man's racehorse," it became the sporting pet of miners in the north of England, where Whippet racing is still very popular. Originally, the dogs raced after live rabbits, but now artificial lures are used instead.

Coat Short, fine, and close.

Color Any color or mixture of colors.

Features Long, lean head; bright, oval-shape eyes with a very alert expression; rose-shape ears; deep chest with plenty of heart-room; tapering tail; no feathering.

Size Height: dogs 18½–20 in, bitches 17½–18½ in. Weight: 28 lb.

Care Needs plenty of exercise. Its short coat requires only a brush and rub-down; better housed indoors year round.

Character A gentle dog and good with children, it makes a fine pet and a splendidly alert watchdog.

Deerhound

One of the most ancient of British breeds, the Deerhound may have arrived in Scotland with Phoenician traders about 3000 years ago, and thereafter developed its thick weather-resistant coat to combat the colder climate.

Coat Shaggy but not overcoated.
Color Dark blue-gray and lighter grays; brindles and yellows; sandy red or red-fawn with black points.

Features Head broadest at ears, tapering toward eyes; dark eyes; ears set on high, folded back in repose; body and general formation that of a Greyhound, with larger size and bone; long tail, thick at root.
Size Height: dogs 30–32 in, bitches 28 in. Weight: dogs 85–110 lb, bitches 75–95 lb.
Care Needs lots of exercise but the minimum of grooming. Best kenneled out of doors.
Character A faithful and devoted pet for the energetic. Gentle in the home, but can kill livestock when its hunting instincts are roused.

Irish Wolfhound

The Irish Wolfhound is the tallest dog in the world, and the national dog of Ireland. Bred to kill wolves, it is thought to be descended from dogs brought by the Celts as they spread across Europe.

Coat Rough and harsh.
Color Gray, steel gray, brindle, red, black, pure white, fawn, or wheaten.
Features Long head carried high; dark eyes; small, rose-shape ears; very deep chest; long, slightly curved tail.
Size Minimum height: dogs 32 in, bitches 30 in. Weight: dogs 120 lb, bitches 105 lb.
Care Brushing and the removal of straggly hairs are all that is required.
Character Can be kenneled out of doors, but its calm temperament grants it a place by the fireside.

Afghan Hound

The Afghan Hound is an ancient breed, said by legend to have been one of the animals taken aboard Noah's Ark at the time of the flood! This member of the Greyhound family, possibly related to the Saluki, has certainly existed for centuries. Its ancestors somehow found their way from their original home in Persia (Iran) to Afghanistan, where the breed undoubtedly developed its long, shaggy coat to withstand the harsh climatic conditions. Its speed and stamina meant that, in its native land, it was used to hunt leopards, wolves, and jackals. It is only in the West that it has become a status symbol.

Coat Long and fine.
Color All colors acceptable.
Features Head long and not too narrow; eyes preferably dark, but golden not debarred; ears set low and well back; level back; tail not too short.
Size Height: dogs 27 in, bitches 25 in. Weight: dogs 60 lb, bitches 50 lb.
Care Requires plenty of exercise. The coat should be groomed with an air-cushioned brush and will soon become matted if it is not given sufficient and regular attention.
Character The Afghan is an elegant, beautiful, and affectionate dog, which is generally good natured but does not tolerate teasing. It is intelligent but somewhat aloof.

The Afghan— a fearless hunter turned elegant status symbol.

Anglo-French Hounds

As its name suggests, the Anglo-French came about through crossings between French medium-size hounds and English hounds. There is also a Great Anglo-French Hound and a Small Anglo-French. The Anglo-French Tricolor is one of the most popular hounds in France. They are usually kept in packs, and used to hunt large and small game.

Coat Short and smooth.
Color *Anglo-French* Tricolor—black, white, and orange: white and black; white and orange. *Great Anglo-French* As for Anglo-French. *Small Anglo-French* Usually tricolor—black, white, and orange; may have black saddle covering upper torso and back.

Features *Anglo-French* Head moderate in size in relation to body; dark eyes; pendulous ears; tail carried low. *Great Anglo-French* Kindly eyes; large, hound-like ears; large, big-boned body; tail carried low. *Small Anglo-French* As for Anglo-French.

Size *Anglo-French* Height: 20 in. Weight: 49–55 lb. *Great Anglo-French* Height at withers: 24–27 in. Weight: 66–71 lb. *Small Anglo-French* Height: 19–22 in.

Care By professional hunt staff.
Character Robust and good-natured hounds, usually kept as one of a pack.

Billy

The Billy was devised in south-west France by Monsieur Hublot du Rivault, for the express purpose of hunting wild boar and deer. He commenced selective breeding in 1888, using the wolf-hunter, the Poitevin, the Céris, a hunber of both wolf and hare, and the Montemboeuf, a large, noble hand that would follow only those animals selected as quarry. He called the new breed Billy after a town of that name.

Coat Short and hard to the touch.
Color White or "café au lait"; white with orange or lemon blanket, or mottling.
Features Large, dark, expressive eyes; rather flat ears, set high for a French hound; very deep narrow chest; long, straight tail, sometimes lightly feathered.
Size Height at shoulders: dogs 24–26 in, bitches 23–25 in. Weight: 55–66 lb.
Care Usually kept in a pack.
Character Tall and intelligent, with exceptional hunting and scenting abilities, and a melodious voice. It is known to be somewhat argumentative with its fellows. Its usually kept in a pack.

Poitevin

The Poitevin was developed in the late 1600s in south-west France as a wolf hunter, possessing great speed, courage, and scenting ability.

Coat Short and glossy.
Color Tricolor with black saddle; tricolor with large black patches; sometimes orange and white or badger-pied.
Features Head long but not exaggerated; large, brown, expressive eyes; medium-width ears; very deep chest: back well muscled and very well coupled; medium-length, fine, smooth tail.
Size Height at shoulders: 24–28 in. Weight: 66 lb.
Care Best looked after by professional hunt staff.
Character Large, distinguished hound, swift and intelligent, but timid and reserved. Happiest in a pack.

Grand Griffon Vendéen

The Griffons Vendéen are French sporting dogs. They occur in a number of varieties of which the Grand Griffon Vendéen is the largest and reputed to be the oldest. It is thought to be a descendant of a white Saint Hubert Hound crossed with a tawny and white Italian bitch, and the resultant dogs were known as the King's White Dogs.

Coat Rough, long, and harsh to the touch, with a thick undercoat.

Color Solid fawn or hare; white with red, fawn, gray, or black markings: bicolor or tricolor.

Features Domed head; large, dark eyes, without white, and with a kindly expression; narrow, supple ears; long, wide back; tail set on high, and strong at the base.

Size Height at shoulders: 24–26 in. Weight: 66–77 lb.

Care Requires a considerable amount of exercise, and regular grooming with brush and comb to prevent its coat from matting.

Character Extremely attractive, intelligent dogs which make good family pets as well as hunters. They are independent and love to wander, so all escape routes should be sealed.

Petit Basset Griffon Vendéen

The Petit Basset Griffon Vendéen is a short-legged, rough-coated hound, developed in the Vendée district of south-west France. It was bred down from the Grand Griffon Vendéen, a larger variety originally used in France for wolf hunting and now used against wild boar.

Coat Rough, long, and harsh to the touch, never woolly or silky; thick undercoat.

Color Solid fawn or hare; white with red, fawn, gray, or black markings: bicolor or tricolor.

Features Head medium length and not too wide; large, dark eyes; narrow, fine, supple ears; deep chest with a prominent sternum; medium-length tail, set on high and strong at base.

Size Height at shoulders: 13½–15 in. Weight: 25–35 lb.

Care Needs little grooming and considers humans its friends.

Character This most attractive animal makes a good family pet provided that it receives plenty of exercise.

Tawny Brittany Basset

The Tawny Brittany Basset originated in Brittany, north-west France. It was developed from the Basset Griffon Vendéen and other short-legged bassets to track over rough terrain, where it is fast and active.

Coat Harsh and close.
Color Golden, wheaten, or fawn; white spot on neck or chest permissible.
Features Moderate-length skull; dark, alert eyes; thin ears set on at eye level; chest quite wide and well let down; tail thick at root and tapering toward the tip.
Size Height: 13–17 in.
Care Requires a generous amount of exercise; coat needs little attention.
Character This short-legged, wire-coated hound has courage and a good nose.

Swiss Hounds

The scenthounds or *laufhunde* of
Switzerland include the Swiss, the
Bernese, and the Lucernese Hound.
The modern Swiss, Bernese, and
Lucernese Hounds are very similar in
abilities, character, and in
appearance, except for color of coat.
They have keen noses, great powers of
endurance, and will work over any
terrain. They make excellent tracking
dogs and are used to hunt a variety of
game, including hare, fox, and deer.

Coat *Swiss and Bernese* Rough and wiry,
with a thick undercoat. *Lucernese* Short and
very dense.

Color *Swiss* White with orange markings.
Bernese Tricolor—white, black, strong tan
markings. *Lucernese* White with gray or blue
speckling and broad dark or black markings.

Features Clean, refined head; long
muzzle; mouth with scissor bite; eyes as dark
as possible; very long ears; long, sloping
shoulders; good-length back, tail not too
long, carried horizontally. *Short-legged
varieties* Medium-size head; mouth with
scissor bite; fairly large eyes with tight lids;
ears long enough to reach tip of nose; body
of good hound type, proportionally built;
medium-length tail, set neither too low nor
too high.

Size Minimum height: 17½ in, generally
18–22 in. *Short-legged varieties* 12–15 in.

Care Need a lot of exercise, and should be
groomed with a hound glove, and a slicker
for the rough-coated varieties.

Character Calm
companions with
strong hunting
instincts; not
suitable as pets.

Jura Hounds

The two varieties of Jura Hound, the Bruno and the Saint Hubert, are both native to the Jura mountains area in western Switzerland, and have a similar origin to the other Swiss hounds which they resemble. Strong, enthusiastic hunters, the Jura Hounds are used mainly against hare. They have a good nose, a strong, clear voice, and can cope with any terrain.

Coat Short.

Color Yellowish or reddish brown, with or without large black saddle; black with tan markings over eyes, on cheeks and on underparts of body; may have white mark on chest.

Features Heavy, domed head; eyelids not close fitting; large, very long ears, set on low and well back: moderate-length tail.

Size Minimum height: 17½ in, generally about 18–22 in.

Care Need plenty of exercise and grooming with a hound glove.

Character Gentle and affectionate hunting companions, but not really suited to life as a household pet.

Ariégeois

The Ariégeois, originating in the Ariège, a French province on the Spanish border, is the result of a crossing between the native medium-size hounds, the Gascon Saintongeois and the Gascony Blue. While not a very fast hound, it does have stamina and a keen nose, and this intelligent, eager worker has hunted hare throughout this century.

Coat Fine and close.

Color Usually white with black markings and small tan spots over eyes; black puppies occasionally occur; rich tan should not be normally encouraged.

Features Long, light, narrow head with no wrinkle or dew lap; dark eyes well open and with a sweet expression; fine supple ears; back generally level and well supported; tail well attached and carried "saber" fashion.

Size Height at shoulders: dogs 22–24 in, bitches 21–23 in. Weight: 66 lb.

Care Requires a lot of exercise. Its short coat requires little attention.

Character Finely built with a calm disposition and friendly expression, and altogether a most pleasant animal.

Great Gascony Blue

The Great Gascony Blue is famed for its ability to pick up a "cold" scent. Descending from the scenting dogs of pre-Roman times, it was probably brought to North America by French explorers in the 17th century, and, in 1785, General Lafayette gave a small pack to George Washington, who also bred them. They were crossed with other American hounds to produce a breed with improved tracking ability and stamina.

Coat Short, smooth, weather resistant, and somewhat coarse.

Color White with black patches and extensive black ticking to give appearance of blue dog; tan markings on head.

Features Large, elongated head; ears set low, elongated and folded; chest deep and slightly rounded; legs long and muscular; tail well set on, slight upward curl.

Size Height: dogs 25–28 in, bitches 23½–25½ in. Weight: 71–77 lb.

Care Requires a great deal of exercise and is not a suitable housepet. It should be groomed regularly and the long ears checked frequently.

Character The Great Gascony Blue has a calm and friendly temperament.

Rhodesian Ridgeback

Named after Rhodesia, now Zimbabwe, in southern Africa, this breed has a ridge of hair growing in the reverse direction down the middle of its back. It is also known as the Lion Dog because packs of them were used to hunt lions.

Coat Short, dense, sleek, and glossy.
Color Light wheaten to red wheaten.
Features Flat skull, broad between ears; round eyes, set moderately well apart; ears set rather high; chest very deep but not too wide: tail strong at root and tapering toward tip.

Size Height at withers: dogs 25–26½ in, bitches 24–26 in. Weight: 66–75 lb.
Care Needs plenty of exercise and daily grooming with a hound glove.
Character Obedient, good with children and will guard its owners with its life. May move suddenly, when it spies a rabbit.

Basenji

The Basenji, which means "bush thing," comes from central Africa. It is famous for being the only dog without a bark.

Coat Short, sleek, close, and very fine.
Color Black, red, or black and tan; all should have white on chest, on feet, and tail tips; white blaze, collar, and legs optional; black and tan with tan melon pips and black, tan, and white mask.
Features Dark, almond-shape eyes; small, pointed ears; well-balanced body with short, level back: tail set on high, curling tightly over spine and lying close to thigh, with a single or double curve.
Size Height: 16–17 in. Weight: 21–24 lb.
Care Needs only a daily rub-down.
Character Playful, loving, and intelligent. Pups may be destructive.

Hamiltonstövare

The Hamiltonstövare, named after Count Adolf Patrick Hamilton, founder of the Swedish Kennel Club. This hound is the most popular hunting hound in its native land.

Coat Strongly weather-resistant upper coat lying close to body; short, close, soft undercoat.

Color Black, brown, and white—upper side of neck,back, sides of trunk, and upper side of tail, black; head, legs, side of neck, trunk, and tail, brown; blaze on upper muzzle, underside of neck, breast, tip of tail, and feet, white; mixing of black and brown undesirable, as is predominance of any one of the three colors.

Features Fine long head, flat; expressive, clear amber eyes; large, thin, stiff ears; level back; long, thin, low-set tail.

Size Height: dogs 19½–23½ in, bitches 18–22½ in. Weight: 50–60 lb.

Care Needs plenty of exercise, and daily grooming using a hound glove.

Character Smart, affectionate, and intelligent dog; a good companion which may be kept in the home.

Elkhound

The Gray Norwegian Elkhound has probably existed in its native Scandinavia for thousands of years. Archaeologists have discovered bones of similar dogs dating back to 5000–4000 BC. Its task was to seek an elk and hold it at bay until its master moved in for the kill.

Coat Close, abundant, and weather-resistant; outer coat coarse and straight, undercoat soft and woolly.

Color Various shades of gray with black tips to hairs on outer coat; lighter on chest, stomach, legs, underside of tail, buttocks, and in a harness mark.

Features Wedge-shape head; slightly oval eyes; ears set high; powerful body; strong tail, set on high.

Size Height at shoulders: dogs 20½ in, bitches 19½ in. Weight: dogs 50 lb, bitches 43 lb.

Care Requires daily brushing and combing, and plenty of exercise.

Character Somewhat willful in youth, but generally a good-natured pet.

Sicilian Hound

The Sicilian Hound, thought to have been brought from Egypt to Sicily over 3000 years ago, is a mysterious, wise-looking hound which is said by some to have supernatural powers.

Coat Harsh to the touch.

Color Any shade of fawn, small white markings acceptable; solid white, or white with orange markings.

Features Long head with oval-shape skull; triangular ears with stiff, straight points, carried erect; body as long as it is high; fairly long tail set on low, without brush or long hair.

Size Height at shoulders: dogs 18–20 in, bitches 17–18 in. Weight: dogs 26–30 lb, bitches 22–26 lb.

Care Coat needs little attention.

Character A quiet hunter with an excellent nose, though primarily a sighthound.

Ibizan Hound

The Ibizan Hound is native to Ibiza, one of the Spanish Balearic Isles, and is descended from ancient Egyptian hunting dogs.

Coat Smooth or rough: hard, close, dense.
Color Solid white, chestnut, or lion, or any combination of these.
Features Long, fine head; flat skull with prominent occipital bone; clear amber, expressive eyes; large, thin, stiff, highly mobile ears; level back; thin tail set on low.

Size Height at withers: dogs 23½–27½ in , bitches 22½–26 in. Weight: dogs 50 lb, bitches 45 lb.
Care Needs a lot of exercise; coat needs daily brushing.
Character Kindly, good with children, rarely fights, and makes a fine gundog or housepet. It has acute hearing, so must never be shouted at.

Pharaoh Hound

The Pharaoh Hound has been described as the oldest domesticated dog in recorded history because it so closely resembles the dogs carved on the tomb walls of the pharaohs and on ancient Egyptian artefacts dating back to at least 2,000 BC.

Coat Short and glossy.
Color Tan or rich tan with white markings; white tip on tail strongly desirable; white star on chest, white on toes, and slim white blaze on center line of face permissible; flecking or white other than above undesirable.

Features Long, lean, well-chiseled head; eyes amber, blending with coat; medium-size ears set high; lithe body with almost straight top line; tail medium set, fairly thick at base, and tapering toward tip, reaching just below point of hock in repose.
Size Height at withers: dogs 22–25 in, bitches 21–24 in.
Care Coat needs little attention; requires plenty of exercise and is not suited to cramped conditions.
Character Happy and confident, it likes children, and makes a good family pet.

Large, erect ears designed to radiate heat betray the Pharaoh Hound's desert origins.

Saluki

The Saluki, which dates back to 3,000 BC, may take its name from the ancient city of Saluk in the Yemen, or from the town of Seleukia in the ancient Hellenic empire in Syria. It is prized by the Bedouin people for hunting gazelle, but elsewhere in the world it is kept as a companion and show dog. It is also known as the Gazelle Hound, the Arab Gazelle Hound, the Eastern Greyhound, and the Persian Greyhound.

Coat Smooth, silky in texture.

Color White, cream, fawn, golden, red, grizzle, silver grizzle, deer grizzle, tricolor (white, black, and tan), and variations of these colors.

Features Long, narrow head; eyes dark to hazel: long, mobile ears, not set too low; fairly broad back; strong hip bones set wide apart; tail set on low from long, gently sloping pelvis.

Size Height: 22–28 in. Weight: 44–66 lb.

Care Requires plenty of exercise; coat needs daily grooming using a brush and hound glove.

Character Elegant, if somewhat aloof. Loyal, affectionate, and trustworthy; its hunting instincts need to be controlled around livestock.

Borzoi

The Borzoi, or Russian Wolfhound, was used in imperial Russia from the 17th century for wolf coursing—the Borzoi tracked the wolf, when it was beaten from cover, but did not kill it. The dog's task was to grab the wolf by the neck and throw it, whereupon it would be killed with a blow from a dagger. Originally there were various strains of Borzoi, including the Sudanese Borzoi, but the strain developed in Russia forms the basis for today's breed standard. The name comes from the Russian word, *borzii*, meaning swift.

Coat Silky, flat, and wavy or rather curly; never woolly.

Color Any color acceptable.

Features Long, lean head, in proportion to overall size; dark eyes with intelligent, alert expression; small, pointed ears; chest deep and narrow; long tail.

Size Minimum height at withers: dogs 29 in, bitches 27 in. Weight: dogs 75–105 lb, bitches 15–20 lb or less.

Care Requires considerable space and exercise. Should be kept away from livestock; coat needs little attention.

Character Elegant, intelligent, and faithful, but a little aloof.

TERRIERS

Bull Terrier

Considered by some the picture of ugliness, the Bull Terrier began life as a cross between an Old English Bulldog and a terrier. It was originally a fighting dog.

Coat Short and flat.
Color For white, pure white coat; for coloreds, brindle preferred; black, red, fawn, and tricolor acceptable.

Features Long, straight head, and deep right to end of muzzle; eyes appear narrow; small, thin ears set close together; short tail, set on low and carried horizontally.
Size Height: 21–22 in. Weight: 52–62 lb.
Care Too strong for other than the able-bodied to handle, and needs careful training. Its short, flat coat is easy to look after.
Character Despite its fierce appearance and strength, it makes a faithful and devoted pet. The bitch, in particular, is utterly reliable with children.

Unique among dog breeds, the Bull Terrier's head shape is set off by naturally erect ears.

Miniature Bull Terrier

A smaller replica of the Bull Terrier, dogs weighing as little as 10 lb were recorded early in its history.

Coat Short, flat, with a fine gloss.
Color Pure white, black, brindle, red, fawn, and tricolor acceptable.
Features Eyes appear narrow, obliquely placed, and triangular in shape; thin ears set close together; very muscular, long, arched neck, tapering from shoulders to head, free from loose skin; short tail, set on low and carried horizontally.

Size Height at shoulders: 10–14 in. Weight: 10–40 lb.
Care Requires daily brushing and plenty of vigorous exercise.
Character Loving and companionable; an excellent, loyal pet and generally good with children.

Staffordshire Bull Terrier

The lovable Staffordshire, or Staffy, derived from crossing an Old English Bulldog and a terrier, at a time when bull-baiting and dog fighting were popular "sports" in Britain. The resultant dogs had the ideal attributes for combat: the strength and tenacity of a bulldog coupled with the agility and quick wits of a terrier. It is not to be confused with the American Staffordshire or Pit Bull Terrier.

Coat Smooth, short, and dense.
Color Red, fawn, white, black, or blue, or any one of these colors with white; any shade of brindle, or any shade of brindle with white.
Features Short, deep, broad skull; eyes preferably dark, but may bear some relation to the coat color; rose or half-pricked ears; close-coupled body; medium-length tail.
Size Height at shoulders: 14–16 in. Weight: dogs 28–38 lb, bitches 24–34 lb.
Care Easy to look after, requiring little other than regular brushing.
Character One of the most popular pets and a fine household dog as well as a guard, being an affectionate and game companion which adores children. However, it is not averse to having a fight with its fellows, usually emerging the victor, and so it is sensible to keep it on the leash while out walking.

Heavily built of almost solid muscle, the Staffordshire Bull Terrier still resembles its ancestors.

Since bull-baiting
and dog fighting
became illegal,
the "Staffy" has
gained popularity
as a family pet.

Fox Terrier

The Smooth Fox Terrier started life as a stable dog, its job being to hunt vermin. It probably descends from terriers in the English counties of Cheshire and Shropshire, with some Beagle blood added. The Wire, which is a great rabbiter, originated in the coal-mining areas of Durham and Derbyshire in England, and in Wales. As their names imply, they will also pursue foxes. For many years, the Smooth and Wire Fox Terriers were bred together, regardless of coat. All the great Wires resulted from the mating of a Smooth Fox Terrier called Jock with a bitch of unknown antecedents, but definitely wire-haired, called Trap. The Smooth was given its own register in 1876, three years after the British Kennel Club was founded, but the conformation of the two breeds remains the same. The Wire is more popular than its smooth-coated relative, which is rarely seen outside the show ring.

Smooth-haired

Wire-haired

Coat *Smooth* Straight, flat, and smooth. *Wire* Dense and very wiry.

Color *Smooth* All white; white with tan or black markings—white should predominate; brindle, red, or liver markings highly undesirable. *Wire* White should predominate with black or tan markings; brindle, red, liver, or slate-blue markings undesirable.

Features *Smooth* Flat, moderately narrow skull; dark, small eyes, rather deep set; small, V-shape ears dropping forward close to cheek; chest deep, not broad; tail customarily docked. *Wire* Top line of skull almost flat; dark, bright eyes; small V-shape ears of moderate thickness; short, strong, level back; tail customarily docked.

Size Maximum height at withers: dogs 15½ in, bitches slightly less. Weight: 15½–17½ lb.

Care The Smooth needs daily grooming with a stiff brush, and trimming and chalking before a show. The Wire needs to be hand-stripped three times a year, and to be groomed regularly.

Character Affectionate and trainable, and an ideal small child's companion.

Irish Terrier

The Irish claim that their national terrier is a smaller version of the Irish Wolfhound and has been in existence in Ireland for centuries. It seems more likely that it is a descendant of wire-haired Black and Tan Terriers, whose job was to repel vermin and hunt some 200 years ago.

Coat Harsh and wiry.
Color Whole-colored, preferably red, red wheaten, or yellow-red; small amount of white on chest acceptable; white on feet or any black shading highly undesirable.

Features Long head, flat and narrow between ears; small, dark, unprominent eyes; small, V-shape ears; deep, muscular tail, customarily docked.
Size Height at shoulders: 18 in. Weight: about 25–27 lb.
Care Coat should be stripped two or three times a year, and it should be groomed and brushed regularly.
Character An expert ratter and gundog, also makes an affectionate pet.

The Irish Terrier resembles a small Airedale, but has a more fiery coat color.

Kerry Blue Terrier

Originating in County Kerry, southwestern Ireland, the Kerry Blue Terrier is an excellent sporting dog and fine swimmer. Its ancestors are thought to have included the Irish, Bedlington, and Bull Terriers. According to legend, it traces its lineage back to a blue terrier which was so ferocious that it killed every opponent. The Kerry Blue is certainly not a dog it is wise to encounter off the lead when exercising a Chihuahua!

Coat Soft, spiky, plentiful, and wavy.

Color Any shade of blue, with or without black points; a small white patch on chest should not be penalized.

Features Eyes as dark as possible; small to medium-size, V-shape ears; short-coupled body with good depth of brisket and well-sprung ribs; tail set on high and carried erect, customarily docked.

Size Height: dogs 18–19½ in, bitches 17½–19 in. Weight: 33–40 lb.

Care Needs daily grooming with a stiff brush and metal-tooth comb.

Character Mainly kept as a pet. It is good with children, while retaining excellent guarding qualities. However, it may display a fierce temper against dogs or other pets when roused.

Airedale Terrier

The Airedale is the king of the terriers, being the largest member of the terrier group. Named after the Valley of Aire in Yorkshire, England, it was the progeny of a working terrier and an Otterhound. It is an expert ratter and duck-catcher, can be trained to the gun, and is also a splendid guard.

Coat Hard, dense, and wiry.

Color Body-saddle, top of neck, and top surface of tail, black or grizzle; all other parts tan; ears often darker, shading may occur round neck and side of skull; white hairs between forelegs acceptable.

Features Long, flat skull; small, dark eyes; V-shape ears; deep chest; short, strong, straight, level back; tails set on high and carried gaily, customarily docked.

Size Height: dogs 23–24 in, bitches 22–23 in. Weight: 44 lb.

Care Needs plenty of exercise; will need to be hand-stripped twice a year for show.

Character As a family pet, it is good with children, extremely loyal, and seems to adapt well to fairly cramped conditions.

The Airedale has a distinguished record in the police, military, and rescue services.

Soft-Coated Wheaten Terrier

One of the oldest native dog breeds of Ireland, the Soft-coated Wheaten Terrier is believed to be a cross of the Irish and Kerry Blue Terriers. Developed to hunt rabbits, rats, and other prey, it will work any kind of covert and no respectable Irish farmer would be without one.

Coat Soft and silky.

Color A good, clear wheaten, the shade of ripening wheat; white and red considered equally objectionable.

Features Head and skull flat and moderately long; clear, bright, dark hazel eyes; V-shape ears; compact body; tail customarily docked.

Size Height at withers: dogs 18–19½ in, bitches slightly less. Weight: 35–45 lb.

Care Revels in plenty of exercise; coat should be groomed regularly using a metal comb and a wire brush.

Character Best indoors as a family pet; gentle, affectionate, and devoted, and generally loves children.

Welsh Terrier

The Welsh Terrier was once popular for hunting badgers, otters, and foxes. Originally, there were two strains: a Celtic strain, using a coarse-haired Black and Tan Terrier, and an English strain, using an Airedale and a Fox Terrier cross. The English strain is said to have died out.

Coat Abundant, wiry, hard, and close.
Color Black and tan for preference; also black, grizzle, and tan; free from black penciling on toes; black below hocks most undesirable.

Features Head flat and moderately wide between ears; small, dark eyes well set in; small, V-shape ears carried forward; short, well ribbed-up body; long, muscular legs; tail well set on but not carried too gaily, customarily docked.
Size Maximum height at shoulders: 15½ in. Weight: 20–21 lb.
Care Enjoys plenty of exercise; many owners have their dog's coat clipped.
Character A fun dog, the Welsh Terrier is energetic, affectionate, and generally good with children.

Lakeland Terrier

The Lakeland Terrier, from the Lake District in England, was developed to protect lambs from foxes. It is thought that the Border, the Bedlington, and the Dandie Dinmont Terriers, and probably later the Fox Terrier, all contributed to the breed. The result is a practical and courageous working animal, resembling an Airedale Terrier in miniature, which is small enough to follow prey underground.

Coat Dense and harsh, with weather-resistant undercoat.

Color Black and tan, blue and tan, red, wheaten, red grizzle, liver, blue, or black; mahogany or deep tan not typical; small tips of white on feet and chest considered undesirable but permissible.

Features Flat skull; refined, dark or hazel eyes; moderately small ears; reasonably narrow chest; tail customarily docked.

Size Height at shoulders: 14½ in. Weight: dogs 17 lb, bitches 15 lb.

Care Needs a fair amount of exercise. Coat requires daily brushing.

Character Has retained its sporting instincts, yet makes an excellent housepet and a smart yet lively guard.

Manchester Terrier

The Manchester Terrier's ancestors were sporting terriers that would kill rats in a pit for the amusement of spectators in the mid-19th century, a sport popular in Manchester and other areas in northern England.

Coat Close, smooth, short, and glossy.
Color Jet black and rich tan.
Features Long, flat, narrow skull; small, dark, sparkling eyes; small, V-shape ears; chest narrow and deep; short tail, set on where arch of back ends.

Size Height at shoulders: dogs 16in, bitches 15 in. Weight: 12–22 lb.
Care The only grooming required is a daily brush and rubdown.
Character Long-lived; a one-person animal, often chosen as companion by older dog-lovers. Also a good family pet.

Norfolk Terrier

Originally classified as a Norwich Terrier, both dogs were probably a mixture of Cairn, Border, and Irish Terriers. The only difference between the Norfolk and Norwich Terriers today is their ears: the ears of the Norfolk are flat and fold forward, while those of the Norwich are upright.

Coat Hard, wiry, and straight.
Color All shades of red, wheaten, black, and tan, or grizzle; white marks and patches undesirable but permissible.

Features Broad skull; deep-set, oval-shape eyes; medium-size, V-shape ears, slightly rounded at tip; compact body; tail-docking optional.
Size Height at withers: 10 in. Weight: about 11–12 lb.
Care Requires daily brushing, and some trimming if it is to be exhibited.
Character Sociable, hardy, and lovable, it is certainly alert and fearless, but good with children. Has an equable temperament and makes a fine household pet.

Norwich Terrier

From 1979, the prick-eared Norwich Terrier has been classified separately from the otherwise identical, drop-eared Norfolk Terrier. It is named after the city of Norwich, eastern England, where it appears to have originated. Both dogs were popular with students at Cambridge University.

Coat Hard, wiry, and straight.
Color All shades of red, wheaten, black and tan, or grizzle; white marks undesirable.
Features Strong, wedge-shape muzzle; small, dark, oval-shape eyes; erect ears set well apart on top of skull; short back; docked tail optional.
Size Height at withers: 10 in. Weight: 10–12 lb.
Care Enjoys regular exercise and needs only a daily brushing.
Character Hardy and adaptable; good with children.

Sealyham Terrier

Named after the village of Sealyham in Wales, where it originated, the Sealyham Terrier goes back to the 15th century, when it was bred to go to ground in the now illegal sport of badger digging.

Coat Long, hard, and wiry, with a weather-resistant undercoat.

Color All white, or white with lemon, brown, blue, or badger pied markings on head and ears; much black or heavy ticking considered undesirable.

Features Head slightly domed; dark, well-set eyes; medium-size ears; medium-length body; tail set in line with back and carried erect, customarily docked.

Size Maximum height at shoulders: 12 in. Weight: dogs 20 lb, bitches 18 lb.

Care Requires regular brushing and must be hand-stripped for the show ring.

Character A fine family pet, good with children, but not averse to a fight.

Scottish Terrier

Bred to dispel vermin, the Scottie has existed for many centuries and taken many different forms. Many people still tend to think that the West Highland White and the Scottish Terriers are one and the same breed.

Coat Sharp, dense, and wiry, with a short, dense, soft undercoat.

Color Black, wheaten, or brindle.

Features Head and skull long without being out of proportion to size of dog; almond-shape eyes: neat, fine-textured ears; well-molded ribs flattening to deep chest; moderate-length tail giving general balance to dog.

Size Height at withers: 10–11 in. Weight: 19–23 lb.

Care Requires daily brushing; beard needs gentle brushing and combing, and coat should be trimmed twice a year.

Character Tends to be a one- or two-person dog. It has a reliable temperament but does not welcome outsiders. It enjoys walks, loves to play ball games, and is thoroughly sporty, home-loving, and independent.

Erect ears and prominent eyebrows on a long face give the Scottie a somewhat stern appearance.

Skye Terrier

Developed to go to ground after badgers, foxes, otters, and rabbits, the Skye Terrier is said to originate from the Isle of Skye in Scotland.

Coat Long, hard, straight, flat, and free from curl, with a short, close, soft, woolly undercoat.

Color Black, dark or light gray, fawn or cream, all with black points.

Features Head and skull long and powerful; brown, preferably dark, eyes; prick or drop ears; long, low body with level back; when tail is hanging, upper part pendulous and lower part thrown back in a curve, when raised looks like extension of the back line.

Size Ideal height at shoulders: dogs 10 in, bitches 9½ in. Weight: 25 lb.

Care Long coat requires a considerable amount of grooming.

Character Suspicious of or uninterested in anyone other than its owners.

West Highland White Terrier

Like other small Scottish terriers, the West Highland White Terrier, or Westie, was originally bred to hunt vermin. In Britain it is among the most popular of pure-bred dogs.

Coat Harsh and free from curl, with a short, soft, close furry undercoat.
Color White.
Features Slightly domed head; eyes set wide apart; small, erect ears, carried firmly; compact body with level back and broad, strong loins; tail 5–6 in long.

Size Height: dogs 11 in, bitches 10 in. Weight: 15–22 lb.
Care Coat requires regular brushing and stripping; trimming required for show.
Character Game and hardy, easy to train, good with children, and suitable for town as well as country.

A game little dog, the Glen of Imaal Terrier is little known outside its home territory.

Glen of Imaal Terrier

This short-legged terrier comes from the Glen of Imaal in County Wicklow, Ireland. Originally used to dispel vermin, including fox and badger, and in dog fights, it is now mainly a family pet or a working terrier on Irish farms.

Coat Medium length and harsh textured, with a soft undercoat.
Color Blue, brindle, or wheaten; all shades acceptable.

Features Head of good width and fair length with a strong foreface; medium-size brown eyes; small ears, rose-shape or pricked when alert, thrown back in repose; powerful jaws; deep, medium-length body; tail strong at root, well set on and carried gaily, docking optional.
Size Height: 14 in. Weight: 35 lb.
Care Maintaining its charming "shaggy dog" appearance requires daily brushing.
Character Affectionate, brave, good with children, and very playful.

Cairn Terrier

This popular Scottish terrier has been known and used for putting down vermin for 150 years or more. It was named after the cairns (a Scottish word denoting a heap or pile of stones), which often harbored mice or rats.

Coat Profuse, harsh, but not coarse, with short, soft, close undercoat.

Color Cream, wheaten, red, gray, or nearly black; brindling acceptable in all these colors; not solid black, solid white, nor black and tan; dark points, such as ears and muzzle, very typical.

Features Small head; eyes set wide apart; small, pointed ears; level back; short, balanced tail, well furnished with hair but not feathery.

Size Height: 9½–12 in. Weight: 13–16 lb.

Care Enjoys plenty of exercise; requires little grooming other than brushing, combing, and removing of excess feathering.

Character Intelligent, lively, affectionate, and effective for getting rid of vermin.

Dandie Dinmont Terrier

The appealing and devoted little Dandie Dinmont Terrier was originally bred to hunt badgers and foxes.

Coat Soft, linty undercoat and harder topcoat, not wiry, crisp to the hand.
Color Pepper (from bluish black to pale silvery gray) or mustard (from reddish brown to pale fawn).
Features Strongly made head, large but in proportion to dog's size; rich, dark hazel eyes; pendulum ears; long, strong, and flexible body; rather short tail.
Size Height at shoulders: 8–11 in. Weight: about 18–24 lb.
Care Happy with as much exercise as its owner is able to provide; easy to groom using a stiff brush and comb, and removing any surplus hair.
Character Affectionate, playful, and intelligent, best as the family's sole pet.

Border Terrier

Originating from the Border country, the area around the boundary between England and Scotland, the Border Terrier was bred in the middle of the 19th century to run with hounds and yet be small enough to bolt the fox from its lair.

Coat Harsh, dense, with close undercoat.
Color Red, wheaten, grizzle and tan, blue and tan.
Features Dark eyes with keen expression; small, V-shape ears; deep, narrow, fairly long body; short tail.
Size Height: 10 in. Weight: dogs 13–15½ lb, bitches 11½–14 lb.
Care Requires little grooming.
Character The smallest of the working terriers, the Border makes a first-class pet. It loves children, is long-lived, will literally walk its owners off their feet, and is also a good watchdog.

German Hunt Terrier

The German Hunt Terrier was probably developed by crossing the English Fox Terrier with the Lakeland Terrier. It is a courageous hunter, which will take on fox and boar as well as small rodents.

Coat *Smooth* Smooth, harsh, dense, and lying flat. *Rough* Harsh and wiry.
Color Black, grayish black, or dark brown with small, even tan markings.

Features Rather heavy head; small, dark eyes set obliquely; V-shape ears, folded so that tips fall forward; long back; tail set on high and carried erect, usually docked.
Size Maximum height at withers: 16 in. Weight: dogs 19½–22 lb, bitches 16–18 lb.
Care Should be kenneled outdoors, can be groomed with a hound glove.
Character Aggressive, not suitable as a pet or with children.

Bedlington Terrier

The Bedlington may look like a lamb, but its past record ranges from poaching to pit fighting. It is believed that the Greyhound or Whippet played a part in its ancestry.

Coat Thick and linty.
Color Blue, liver, or sandy, with or without tan; darker pigment to be encouraged; blues, and blue and tans must have black noses; livers and sandies must have brown noses.
Features Narrow skull; small, bright, deep-set eyes; moderate-size, filbert-shape ears; muscular body; moderate-length tail, thick at root and tapering to a point.
Size Height at withers: dogs 16–17½ in, bitches 15–16½ in. Weight: 18–22 lb.
Care Needs space, enjoys average exercise, and coat needs regular trimming.
Character Lovable, full of fun, and a terror when provoked. Easy to train and adores children.

Parson Jack Russell Terrier

Bred by a hunting parson to run with hounds and bolt the fox from its lair, the Jack Russell is still in demand as a working terrier and boisterous household pet.

Coat Smooth, or rough and broken.
Color Entirely white or with tan, lemon, or black markings, preferably confined to head and root of tail.
Features Strong-boned head; almond-shape eyes; V-shape ears; strong hindquarters; tail is customarily docked.
Size Height at withers: dogs 13–14 in, bitches 12–13 in.
Care Requires little grooming.
Character An extremely good working terrier, and popular as a household pet with many people, including the elderly. Can be excitable and better suited to being the companion of an active child.

Czesky Terrier

The Czesky or Bohemian Terrier is a short-legged terrier, little known outside its native home of the Czech Republic. It was developed in the middle of this century by crossing the Scottish, the Sealyham, and possibly other terriers. The result is a tough, sturdy dog that will go to ground after quarry, and is an excellent ratter and a fearsome guard.

Coat Fine and silky, with tendency to curl.
Color Blue-gray or light brown, with light markings.
Features Long head; deep-set eyes; pendent ears; sturdy body; tail 7–8 in long, carried horizontally when terrier is excited.
Size Height at shoulders: 11–14 in. Weight: 13–20 lb.
Care Requires plenty of exercise, the occasional visit to the grooming parlor, and a good daily brushing.
Character Fine working terrier; its equable temperament makes it a good children's companion.

Australian Terrier

Reputed to be an unsurpassed vermin killer, which can also dispose of a snake, the Australian Terrier is often mistaken for a large Yorkshire Terrier—and it is considered to be the result of mating Yorkshire and Cairn Terriers.

Coat Harsh, straight, dense, and long, with short, soft undercoat.

Color (A) Blue, steel blue, or dark gray-blue with rich tan (not sandy) on face, ears, under body, lower legs, and around the vent (puppies excepted); top-knot blue or silver, of a lighter shade than leg color. (B) Clear sandy or red; smuttiness or dark shadings undesirable; top-knot a lighter shade.

Features Long head with flat skull, and powerful jaw; small eyes; small, erect, pointed ears; body long in proportion to height; tail set on high, customarily docked.

Size Height at withers: dogs 10–11 in. Weight: 14 lb.

Care Needs only a good daily grooming with a bristle brush; may be kept in or out of doors.

Character Alert, hardy, and devoted family pet.

TOY DOGS

Affenpinscher

The smallest of the pinschers and schnauzers, its name comes from its monkey-like face (the German word *Affe* means "monkey"). It is also known as the Zwergaffenpinscher, or dwarf pinscher, and in France, as the Diabletin Moustache ("the mustached little devil"). It resembles the Griffon Bruxellois, but whether it was the Griffon that contributed to the Affenpinscher or vice versa is a matter of debate.

Coat Rough and thick.

Color Preferably black, but gray shading considered permissible.

Features Slightly undershot jaw; small, high-set ears, preferably erect, but neat drop-ear permissible; round, dark, sparkling eyes; short, straight back; high-set tail, docked in some countries.

Size Height: 9½–11 in. Weight: 6½–9 lb.

Care Thick coat benefits from daily, careful brushing.

Character Appealing, naturally scruffy-looking toy dog, intelligent, and exceedingly affectionate. Makes a good watchdog.

Maltese

A member of the bichon family, this small, white dog is one of the oldest lap dogs, popular with men and women. It has existed on the island of Malta for centuries, and also found its way to China and the Philippines via Maltese traders.

Coat Long, straight coat, silky texture.

Color White; slight lemon markings on ears permissible.

Features Slightly rounded, broad skull; well-defined stop; slightly tapered muzzle; long, well-feathered ears; oval eyes; compact body; long, plumed tail carried high, arched over back.

Size Height at withers: not exceeding 10 in. Weight: 4–6 lb, not exceeding 7 lb.

Care Requires daily grooming with a bristle brush.

Character Happy, healthy, long-lived; a lovable pet.

Löwchen

Established in Spain, France, and Germany since the 16th century, the Löwchen, or Little Lion Dog, featured in Goya's portrait of the Duchess of Alba. Traditionally given a lion clip, similar to that sported by the exhibition poodle, the Löwchen does look like a lion in miniature, complete with mane and tufted tail.

Coat Moderately long and wavy.
Color Any color or combination of colors considered permissible.
Features Wide, short skull; long pendent ears, well fringed; round, dark eyes with intelligent expression; short, strong body; medium-length tail, clipped to resemble a plume or feather duster.
Size Height at withers: 10–13 in. Weight: 8–18 lb.
Care Requires daily brushing.
Character Affectionate, intelligent, and lively; a good pet.

Yorkshire Terrier

The Yorkshire Terrier, or Yorkie, is a comparatively recent breed, having been developed in Yorkshire, England, within the last hundred years or so as a cross of a Skye Terrier and the now extinct Black and Tan Terrier. The Maltese and Dandie Dinmont may also have contributed. Today, this lively little terrier is one of the most popular toy breeds in the world. Alongside the Chihuahua, it is one of the world's smallest dogs, but there are many larger specimens, which are admirably happy and healthy, and make good pets.

Coat Glossy, fine, and silky.

Color Dark steel blue (not silver blue) extending from back of head to root of tail, never mingled with fawn, bronze, or dark hairs; face, chest, and feet rich, bright tan.

Features Small head, flat on top; medium-size, dark, sparkling eyes; small V-shape ears carried erect; compact body; tail usually docked to medium length.

Size Height: about 9 in. Weight: not exceeding 7 lb.

Care Intricate grooming takes much time and effort.

Character Suited to town or country and, like most small terriers, utterly fearless. This bossy, inordinately affectionate and lively little dog makes a fine pet.

The popularity of the "Yorkie" is quite disproportionate to its small size.

English Toy Terrier

The English Toy Terrier was developed from the smallest specimens of Manchester Terriers, which is why it is also known as Toy Manchester Terrier. It has retained its ancestor's ability to hunt vermin.

Coat Thick, close, and glossy.
Color Black and tan.
Features Long, narrow head; dark to black eyes; ears candle flame shape and slightly pointed at tips; compact body; tail thick at root and tapering to a point.

Size Height at shoulders: 10–12 in. Weight: 6–9 lb.
Care Easy to care for, requiring little more than a daily brushing and a rub-down to give its coat a sheen.
Character Affectionate and intelligent, it is good with children but tends to be a one-person dog.

Australian Silky Terrier

The Australian Silky Terrier owes its existence to the cross-breeding of Skye and Yorkshire terriers, and of the Yorkshire and Australian terriers.

Coat Straight, fine, and glossy.

Color Blue and tan, gray, blue and tan with silver-blue top-knot. Tips of hairs should be darker at roots.

Features Small, compactly built dog with body slightly longer than height; head medium length; eyes small, dark, round; ears small, V-shape; tail customarily docked.

Size Average height: 9 in. Weight: 8–10 lb.

Care Needs good daily walks to work off its energy, and regular brushing.

Character Not averse to vermin hunting, it is an affectionate dog.

Brussels Griffon
(and Petit Brabançon)

The Brussels Griffon was once kept by Brussels cab drivers to rid their stables of vermin. It became a companion breed by virtue of its appealing character. The smooth-coated Petit Brabançon probably owes its existence to the introduction of pug blood.

Coat *Brussels Griffon* Harsh, wiry. *Petit Brabançon* Soft, smooth.

Color Red, black, or black and rich tan with white markings.

Features Head, large in comparison to body, rounded, in no way domed, wide between the ears; eyes black rimmed, very dark; body, short back, level from withers to tail root, neither roaching nor dipping; tail, customarily docked short, carried high.

Size Height: 7–8 in. Weight: 5–11 lb, most desirable 6–10 lb.

Care The coat of the rough requires a lot of attention; coats may be clipped.

Character Intelligent and cheerful. Makes a fine companion.

Pug

Originally from China, the Pug is a Mastiff in miniature—sturdy despite its small size. It is believed to have been introduced into Britain in 1688 by William, Prince of Orange, and enjoyed unrivaled status at that time.

Coat Fine, smooth, short, and glossy.
Color Silver, apricot, fawn, or black; black mask and ears, and black trace along back.

Features Ears either "Rose ear"—a small drop ear that folds over and then back—or "Button ear"—the ear flap folds forward with the tip lying close to the head; very large, dark eyes; short, thick-set body; tail set high and tightly curled over the back.
Size Height: 10–12 in. Weight: 14–18 lb.
Care Requires only modest exercise, but over-exertion should be avoided in very hot weather. Daily grooming with a brush and a rub-down with a silk handkerchief will make its coat shine.
Character Happy, intelligent dog, good with children.

Pomeranian

A member of the spitz family from the Arctic Circle, the Pomeranian was bred down from white spitz that existed in Pomerania, northern Germany, from about 1700.

Coat Long, straight, and harsh, with a soft, fluffy undercoat.

Color All colors permissible, but free from black or white shadings; whole colors are white, black, brown, light or dark blue.

Features Head and nose soft in outline; medium-size eyes; small, erect ears set not too low down or too wide apart; short back and compact body; tail set high, turns over back, and is carried flat and straight.

Size Height: not exceeding 11 in. Weight: about 3–7 lb.

Care Double coat may be groomed with a stiff brush every day and regularly trimmed.

Character With a reputation as a lapdog, adores lots of attention; lively and robust, affectionate and faithful.

The Papillon's prominent ears are balanced by a plumed tail.

Papillon

The name Papillon, French for butterfly, comes from the breed's erect ears. This toy spaniel originated in Spain and is believed to be a descendant of the 16th-century Dwarf Spaniel.

Coat Long, abundant, flowing, and silky in texture.

Color White with patches of any color except liver; tricolors—black and white with tan in spots over eyes and inside ears, on cheeks, and under root of tail.

Features Head slightly rounded; large, erect ears carried obliquely like spread butterfly wings; fairly long body with level top-line; long, well-fringed tail.

Size Height at withers: 8–11 in.

Care Easy to look after, needing only a daily brushing to keep the coat shining.

Character Intelligent, healthy, and generally obedient.

Japanese Chin

For more than 1,000 years, this little dog was a favorite of Japanese emperors who decreed that it should be worshipped. It is said that smaller Chins were sometimes kept in hanging cages like pet birds.

Coat Profuse coat; long, soft, and straight.
Color White and black, or white and red, and white (all shades, including sable, lemon and orange); never tricolor.

Features Large round head in proportion to size of dog; short muzzle; small ears, set wide apart; large dark eyes; square, compact body; well-feathered tail set high and curling over back.
Size Weight (ideal): 4–7 lb.
Care Requires an average amount of exercise and little grooming, except for a daily going over with a pure-bristle brush. Avoid exertion in hot weather.
Character A popular show dog. Attractive and hardy, good with children.

The Japanese Chin probably shares a common ancestor with the Pekingese and the Pug.

Pekingese

The origins of the Pekingese may be traced back some 1,500 years. Believed to be a close relative of the Lhasa Apso and the Shih Tzu, they were said to combine the nobility of the lion with the grace and sweetness of the marmoset. Favored by the 19th-century Chinese Imperial court, they were so prized that no commoner was allowed to own one.

Coat Long and straight, double-coated with coarse top coat, thick undercoat; profuse mane and feathered tail.

Color All colors and marking are permissible and of equal merit, except albino or liver. Particolors should be evenly broken.

Features Wide, flat head with shortened muzzle and deep stop; flat face; prominent round eyes; feathered ears carried close to head; thick chest and neck, short body with slightly rolling gait; tail set high and curving over back.

Size Weight: dogs, not exceeding 11 lb; bitches not exceeding 12 lb.

Care Requires considerable brushing and frequent combing.

Character A thickset, dignified little dog with a mind of its own; intelligent and fearless, its ideal role is that of a pampered companion.

King Charles Spaniel

Also known as the English Toy Spaniel—the name "King Charles" being reserved for the Black and Tan variety only—the King Charles Spaniel's history can be traced back to Japan in 2,000 BC.

Coat Long, silky, straight coat. Slight waviness permissible.

Color *Black and Tan* Raven black with bright tan markings above eyes, on cheeks, inside ears, on chest and legs, and underside of tail; white marks undesirable. *Ruby* Solid rich red, white markings undesirable. *Blenheim* Rich chestnut markings, well broken up, on pearly white ground; markings evenly divided on head, leaving room for lozenge spot between ears. *Tricolor* Black and white, well spaced and broken up with tan markings over eyes, cheeks, inside ears, inside legs, on underside of tail.

Features Large domed skull, full over eyes; deep, well-defined stop; low-set ears, long and well feathered; wide, deep chest; well-feathered tail, carried above level of back; docked in the USA.

Size Height: 10 in. Weight: 8–14 lb.

Care Should be brushed every day with a bristle brush; eyes should be kept clean with veterinary eye wipes.

Character A delightful pet, good with children, and full of fun.

This toy breed owes its name to the affection King Charles II developed for it.

Cavalier King Charles Spaniel

The Cavalier is very similar to the King Charles Spaniel, but while the King Charles has an apple-domed head, the slightly larger Cavalier is almost flat between the ears and its stop is shallower. Both breeds were named after King Charles II (1630–85), and the Cavalier was the original favorite.

Coat Long and silky, free from curl.

Color *Black and Tan* Black with bright tan marks above eyes, head, chest, legs, underside of tail; white marks undesirable. *Ruby* Rich red; white markings undesirable. *Blenheim* Chestnut markings, well broken up, on white ground; markings evenly divided on head, lozenge between ears. *Tricolor* Black and white, well spaced and broken up, with tan markings over head, inside legs, on underside of tail.

Features Flattish skull; long ears, set high; large, dark eyes; short-coupled body; long, well-feathered tail.

Size Weight: 12–18 lb.

Care Enjoys a fair amount of exercise; should be groomed every day.

Character Good natured and generally fond of children.

Chihuahua

The Chihuahua is believed to have been a sacred dog of the Aztecs. However, a dog not unlike it may well have existed in Egypt some 3,000 years ago. Early Chihuahuas were slightly larger and had bigger ears than modern ones, which may be the result of a cross with the hairless Chinese Crested Dog. There are two varieties of Chihuahua, the Smooth-coated and Long-coated, the latter having long hair of soft texture, which is either flat or slightly wavy.

Coat *Long coat* Long and soft to touch, slight waviness permissible. *Smooth coat* Short and dense, soft to touch.
Color Any color or mixture.
Features Apple-domed head; large flaring ears; large, round eyes that do not protrude; level back; medium length, high set tail, curved over back.
Size Height: 6½–8 in. Weight: up to 6 lb.
Care Inexpensive to keep, and both long-haireds and short-haireds are fairly easy to groom, requiring only daily combing and brushing with a soft brush.

Character Exceedingly intelligent, affectionate, possessive, and a good watchdog in miniature. Care must be taken on outings that it does not start a fight because it seems to imagine that it is enormous when confronted with other, much bigger canines.

The Chihuahua, the world's
smallest dog, is named
after the Mexican state.

At one time the two varieties of
Chihuahua—Long-coated and
Smooth-coated—were allowed to
interbreed, but this is no longer
acceptable.

Italian Greyhound

There is little doubt that the Italian Greyhound is a descendant of the Greyhound, one of the most ancient breeds in the world. It may have been the first breed to have been developed exclusively as a companion or pet.

Coat Short, fine, and glossy.

Color Solid black, blue, cream, fawn, red or white, or any of these colors broken with white; white broken with one of above colors; black or blue with tan markings, or brindle, not acceptable.

Features Long, flat, and narrow skull; slight stop; rose-shape ears, set well back; large, expressive eyes; hare feet; low-set long tail, carried low.

Size Height at withers: 12½–15 in. Weight: 5½–10 lb.

Care Very sensitive, it feels the cold, can be wounded by harsh words, and its legs are all too easily broken. Enjoys exercise, but must have a warm coat in wintry conditions. Easy to groom, a rub-down with a silk handkerchief making its coat shine.

Character Delightful and affectionate, easy to train, rarely molts, and is odorless. Indeed, it has been publicized as the ideal pet.

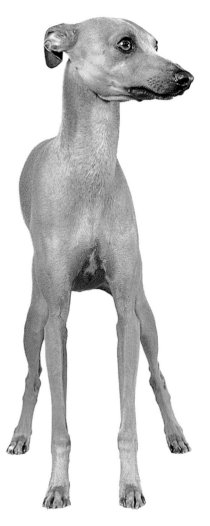

Miniature Pinscher

The Miniature Pinscher, or Min Pin as it is commonly called, is known in its native Germany as the Zwergpinscher. It is not a small Doberman but the cross of a German Pinscher with an Italian Greyhound and, it is thought, Dachshund.

Coat Hard, smooth, short coat.
Color Black, blue or chocolate, with sharply defined tan markings on cheeks, lips, lower jaws, throat, twin spots above eyes and cheeks, lower half of forelegs, inside of hind legs and vent region, lower portion of nodes and feet.

Features Tapering narrow skull; small, erect or drop ears set on high; bright dark eyes; compact, square body; tail set high, level with topline, often docked.
Size Height at withers: 10–12 in. Weight: about 10 lb.
Care Easy to groom, requiring little more than a daily brush and a rub-down with a silk handkerchief or piece of chamois leather to make its coat shine.
Character Ideal pet for town or country, being affectionate and intelligent, and rarely molting.

The broad chest and muscular legs enable the feet to be lifted high in the characteristic hackney gait.

Chinese Crested Dog

The almost hairless Chinese Crested is said to have originated in China and been taken to South America in Chinese sailing ships many centuries ago. It has no coat except for a flowing crest or mane, and hair on its feet and plumed tail. However, in almost every litter, there are some haired pups which grow into luxuriantly coated adults resembling little sheepdogs. These are known as Powder Puffs.

Coat *Chinese Crested Hairless*: Tuft of long, soft hair only on head, feet, and tail. *Chinese Crested Powder Puff*: Double, long, straight outer coat, soft silky undercoat.
Color Any color or combination.
Features Slightly rounded head and skull; low-set erect ears; dark eyes; body may be racy and fine-boned (deer type) or heavier (cobby type); slender tapering tail set high and carried forward over the back in motion.
Size Height: dogs 11–13 in, bitches 9–12 in. Weight: not exceeding 12 lb.
Care Food rations should be increased in the winter months. Should be bathed about every three weeks and have its skin massaged with cream. Adjusts to warm or cold climates but should *never* be kenneled out of doors; must be protected against sun.
Character An excellent pet, frequently hyperactive, playing tirelessly, and leaping about in anticipation of food.

For show purposes, the hair on the Chinese Crested may be long or short, but a full crest on the head and a full plume on the tail are preferred.

The Powder Puff
Chinese Crested
Dog takes its
name from the
silky double coat,
which makes its
ears drop
forward.

INDEX